Torres
el Niño my story

Fernando Torres

with Antonio Sanz

HarperSport
An Imprint of HarperCollins*Publishers*

Contents

I   Mersey reds   12
II   Why I am an atlético   24
III   My debut   34
IV   My life in Madrid   44
V   The cathedral: Anfield   54
VI   The men who made Liverpool great: 66
VII   The captain's armband   78
VIII Living in Liverpool   88
IX   A day of football   98
X   'Spanish' Liverpool   108
XI   A bitter taste   118
XII   Adiós, Atlético   128
XIII Rafa's way   138
XIV   Through the lens   148
XV   First act: Chelsea at Anfield   160
XVI   The best league in the world   170
XVII My Champions League bow   182
XVIII Meeting in Madrid   194
XIX   Fortress Melwood   206
XX   A helping hand   218
XXI   Suffering in silence   228
XXII Champions in Vienna   238
XXIII On the podium in Zurich   254
XXIV Switching off   266
XXV   I'll never walk alone   276

Photographic Acknowledgements   288

First published in 2009 by
HarperSport
an imprint of HarperCollins
77-85 Fulham Palace Road
London W6 8JB

1

A CIP catalogue record for this book is available from the British Library

ISBN 978-0-00-732379-1

Translated from Spanish to English by Sid Lowe

Printed and bound in Great Britain by Butler Tanner & Dennis, Frome

The HarperCollins website address is www.harpercollins.co.uk

Mixed Sources
Product group from well-managed forests and other controlled sources
www.fsc.org Cert no. SW-COC-001806
© 1996 Forest Stewardship Council

FSC is a non-profit international organisation established to promote the responsible management of the world's forests. Products carrying the FSC label are independently certified to assure consumers that they come from forests that are managed to meet the social, economic and ecological needs of present and future generations.

Find out more about HarperCollins and the environment at
www.harpercollins.co.uk/green

To the best fans
in the world

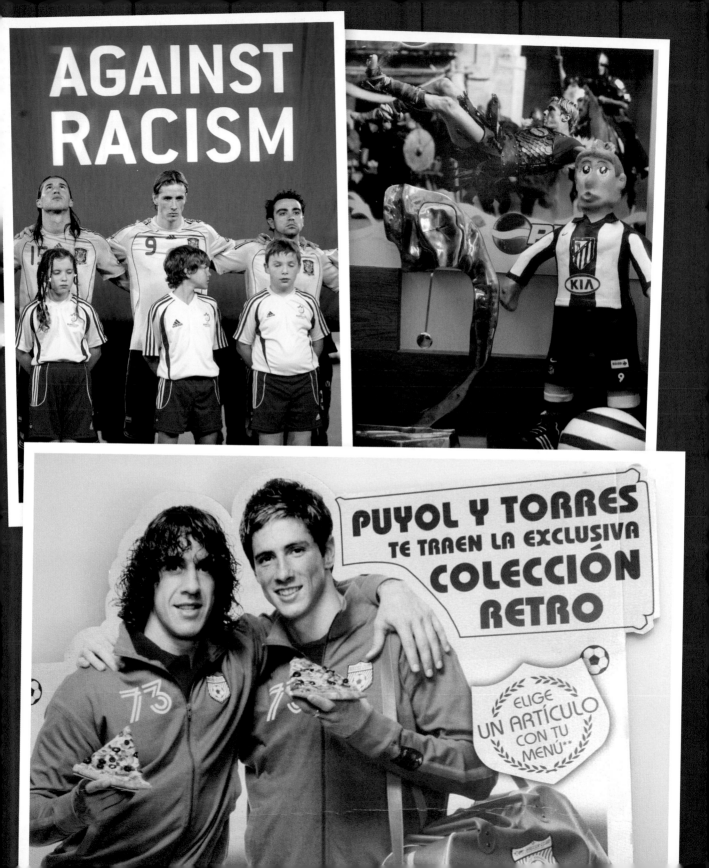

I

Mersey Reds

It happened in San Sebastián, in
northern Spain, when I was playing for
Atlético Madrid against Real Sociedad.
I was battling with a defender,
and the captain's armband I was
wearing came loose and fell open.
As it hung from my arm, you
could see the message written
on the inside, in English.

We'll Never Walk Alone.

𝕴t wasn't what I had intended but right there and then I became identified with Liverpool. I hadn't planned for it, and a future at Anfield hadn't even crossed my mind, but that moment of chance, that accident, came to symbolise the next big step in my career: my captaincy at Atlético gave way to the words that define Liverpool.

All of my best friends have the words tattooed on their arms. We were eating together once and they suggested that I do the same. I told them I couldn't. 'You'll Never Walk Alone' is a phrase so intimately linked to one of Europe's biggest clubs, so clearly associated with Liverpool, that I didn't think it was a good idea. I was an Atlético player and a *rojiblanco* through and through. They decided to give me a new captain's armband for my birthday with the phrase on the inside so that, even if I wouldn't get it tattooed on my arm, the phrase would accompany me. My friends would accompany me; we would never walk alone. I gave the armband to the Atlético kit man, who kept it with the team's shirts. When it slipped down that day against Sociedad, an eagle-eyed photographer snapped the picture and I was immediately linked to Liverpool.

Maybe that was the day I took my first step towards Anfield, or maybe it was because I already shared things with Liverpool. I identify with the values that define the club: hard work, struggle, humility, sacrifice, effort, tenacity, commitment, togetherness, unity, faith, the permanent desire to improve, to overcome all obstacles … Once a week Liverpool fans feel like the most important people on earth and make the players feel like it too. They give everything and they ask for nothing in return. Liverpool FC is a club that despite being used to winning

never succumbs to the temptation to start cruising. If you play well the fans enjoy it, and if you play badly they help you get over it. The Liverpool family have helped me off the pitch too. It's as if you live in a neighbourhood where everyone knows you and everyone joins forces for the same cause: the team. Good people, honourable people, who have always got back on their feet however many times destiny has knocked them down. The harder things have been, the more united they have become.

I never imagined I would play for Liverpool. The first rumours about my future started just after I'd played in the Nike Cup in Italy at the age of fifteen. That was May 1999 and the newspaper *Marca* started to link me to Arsenal. The only thing I was worried about then was passing my exams and enjoying my summer holiday in Galicia. But the Premier League bug did bite. A couple of years later, just after I had made my debut for the Atlético first team, there was talk about Manchester United. Back then, Liverpool wasn't an option at all but other clubs were. A scout from Arsenal even contacted me and gave me his card in case I wanted to have a trial with the Gunners.

My interest in the Premier League grew. In Spain, most people only ever talked about La Liga. At the time there was little coverage of foreign leagues and few Spanish players were playing their club football outside the country. That was the time, in the late 1990s, when Arsenal built a great side with Dennis Bergkamp, Ian Wright, David Seaman, Tony Adams, Nicolas Anelka and a very young Thierry Henry, with Arsène Wenger as coach. They were wonderful to watch. So much so that I used to choose Arsenal when I played *chapas* – the Spanish equivalent of table football played with bottle tops. You would play against friends with metal bottle tops that you painted in the colours of your favourite team; I'd painted mine Arsenal colours with the players' names on. We would challenge each other to games at school and in the parks in Fuenlabrada, the town just outside Madrid where I lived. When José Antonio Reyes signed for them, I followed with interest: I kept a close eye on his progress, his team-mates, and his new club.

I had always been interested in foreign leagues as a kid. I followed the Italian league as much as possible because I loved the way that the Argentinians Gabriel Batistuta and Abel Balbo played. I also liked a kid that was coming through by the name of Francesco Totti. Before that I remember Arrigo Sacchi's Milan, van Basten in particular, and later I followed Juventus with Alessandro Del Piero, Gianluca Vialli and Fabrizio Ravanelli. Then there was George Weah at Milan, a phenomenal player. My favourite in Italy was always Batistuta. He had everything. But my idol at home was Kiko Narváez – one of the heroes of the league and cup double that Atlético won in 1996.

In the summer of 2006 after the World Cup in Germany, Bahía Internacional, the company that have looked after me since I was fifteen, told me that there had been discussions with Manchester United. Sir Alex Ferguson had been involved in the negotiations but in the end nothing happened: maybe neither of us really pushed hard enough.

I also found out that some other English clubs, like Newcastle and Tottenham, had made offers which Atlético rejected – just as they did to offers from Olympique Lyon and Inter Milan. I also felt that it wasn't the time to leave and none of the offers entirely convinced me. My desire to succeed with Atlético stopped me thinking about a change.

When Liverpool's offer arrived a year later, I took a long time thinking about it and in the end I decided it was time for a change. I felt that I was stagnating in Spain and that my development was grinding to a halt. The Premier League is the strongest in Europe. A few years ago, La Liga was the best but the huge influx of foreign players has allowed the English league to improve and the football is more attractive now – it's faster and more intense, there are more goal scoring chances and the players respect the rules of the game better. In England, players don't dive. They try to help the referees, they don't try to take advantage of every situation and the game isn't constantly stopping. There's a level of respect that lets you really enjoy the game. Of course there are tough tackles, but they are honest attempts to win the ball and players who do get fouled get up straight away, even if it hurts, instead of rolling round the turf to try to get the crowd going and put pressure on the referee. As a spectator, I really enjoy watching Premier League games. Even before I signed, my Spanish team-mates – people like Xabi Alonso and Pepe Reina – told me that I would enjoy playing in England even more than I had enjoyed playing in Spain.

I always thought that I would play at Anfield as a visitor, never as part of the home team. I would compare the old Highbury to Anfield; I would have loved to have played there. That respect for history and tradition is something that should be applauded. Reyes and Cesc Fabregas told me about the reverence shown during the final few games at Arsenal's old ground. It's like Anfield, a cathedral to the game. You want to be able to tell your friends: 'I've been there, where so many glorious pages of footballing history were written.'

'Destiny seemed to have decided that if I ever left Atlético Madrid it would be for Liverpool. Having turned down various proposals, Rafa Benítez's call made me reflect and start to have doubts for the first time. I decided that it was the right moment to leave and I asked Miguel-Ángel Gil Marín, Atlético's owner, to listen to Liverpool's offer.'

I didn't know that Liverpool was the most successful club in England. Since Rafa went to Anfield and took Spanish players with him, I had got to know Liverpool better but I didn't realise that. I remember the 2001 Uefa Cup final against Alavés but I thought they were some way behind the teams that I assumed dominated English football: Manchester United and Arsenal. I was surprised when I found out just how incredible their history was and how many titles they had won.

Istanbul revealed Liverpool's true spirit. The Spanish television channel Canal Plus broadcast a report about the history of the club after they had won their fifth European Cup in Turkey – about the tragedies at Heysel and Hillsborough, the connection between players and fans, the struggle against adversity. The commitment to overcome difficulties and stand tall, the ability to face up to every situation and beat it, is reserved for true giants. Liverpool FC is a special and complete club, one that plays and fights, that gives everything for the people who follow it.

I had heard the names that are most associated with Liverpool: Dalglish, Rush, Souness, Keegan, Owen, Fowler, McManaman, Hamann … As someone who has always followed those players who come through the ranks at their clubs, I was especially interested in a young lad from the youth team called Steven Gerrard. In the 1980s Liverpool were practically invincible. I was told that the European ban they suffered after Heysel made them stronger domestically, even though they had an important handicap with less of a presence on the international club stage. You still find Liverpool fans all over the world though and I think the club needs to keep growing by encouraging that and making sure they continue to be known worldwide. Until I signed for Liverpool, I never knew they were so big. And I felt like they didn't have much of a presence beyond

Torres
el Niño

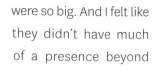

Liverpool's European Cup successes set them apart internationally.

Merseyside either; attention was focused on London and Manchester. But then, suddenly, Liverpool were back in the spotlight. A lot of that is down to Rafa Benítez, who has changed things at the club and revived some of the old Liverpool philosophy, giving the club a global presence again.

Liverpool's two Champions League finals remain fresh in my mind. In Istanbul and Athens the values that embody the club shone through. I turned off the television at half-time in the 2005 final. It seemed to be all over. Everything pointed to the second half being a waste of time, just an exercise in running down the clock. But when I got to the restaurant where I'd arranged to meet with friends, I asked them to put the television on and I couldn't believe it. I don't know where they found the strength and character to take that game into extra-time and penalties. When Liverpool got to the final in Greece two years later, I watched the whole game at home. After what had happened the first time, I wasn't going to miss a minute. I wanted Liverpool to win because I had friends in the team. Once again, things looked bleak but when Dirk Kuyt scored I thought that another comeback was possible. In fact, I'm convinced that if the referee hadn't cut the game short by a few seconds, the Reds would have taken things into extra-time again. The equaliser was possible and a victory likely.

Watching those two nights unfold on television taught me my first lesson about the club I would later join: at Liverpool, no one gives up and everything's possible.

II
Why I'm an atlético

It was a cold winter afternoon, just after Christmas. We had eaten in Dehesa de la Villa, the neighbourhood in Madrid where my grandparents lived, and during the meal someone asked: 'Can we go and see Atlético play?'

They were playing at home against Compostela. It was the perfect game for us, a combination of our commitment to the red and white of Atlético and the pull of home – my father is from a small village near Santiago de Compostela in Galicia, up in the northwest of Spain. My grandfather Eulalio and my father started talking about it, and before I knew it I was sitting in the back of the family car, seat belt across my chest, heading for the banks of the Manzanares river – to the neighbourhood of La Arganzuela where the Vicente Calderón stadium stands.

It wasn't just another day for me. It was the first time I had been to see Atlético Madrid live. Together with my grandfather – my inspiration when it came to supporting Atlético – and my father, we bought three tickets to see a side that was anything but consistent. It all started at 5pm on 15 January 1995 and ended 1–1. Abadía opened the scoring for Compostela and 'The Train' Valencia, our Colombian centre-forward, equalised. I remember watching Caminero, Simeone, Solozábal and López ... players who would go on to win an historic double the following season.

I wasn't hooked when I left the stadium. It was cold, there wasn't much excitement and the flat atmosphere in the stands didn't help. The draw meant I left as I had arrived, without really catching the bug.

And yet with every passing day I felt happier that I had chosen Atlético. I was fast becoming an *atlético* like my grandfather. I felt it. And, just as I saw my first game at the age of ten, a few months later, in July 1995, I had my first trial to play for them, having previously played for a team called Rayo 13 in Fuenlabrada. After signing up and being selected for the trial, I went along with my father and my brother Isra. The trial was held on the gravel pitches in Parque de las Cruces in the neighbourhood of Las Águilas in the south of the city. It was a summer afternoon, a Saturday at 3pm. My father had driven down there earlier in the day to check it out and make sure we didn't get lost en route but we still managed to turn up a couple of hours early.

'You've been selected,' he said, deadpan. 'They've picked six kids and you're one of them. You have to go to Colegio Amorós in the first week of September for another trial to confirm everything.'

The trial consisted of eleven-a-side games split into two twenty-minute halves. There were a lot of kids and not much time. It wasn't exactly an ideal way to prove yourself but things went well for me. I scored a lot of goals and I was very happy with the way I played. Amongst those choosing which kids would be selected were some of the club's legends, men I would later spend years training with like Víctor Peligros and Manolo Briñas. At the end of the trial they told us that the kids who were chosen would be on a list they'd post at the Calderón in mid-August. It wasn't something that obsessed me, far from it. At that age I don't think failure is something that scares you. If I didn't get chosen I would have just gone back to playing football in my neighbourhood, happy as I had ever been.

Time went by and the family holiday in Galicia meant that we couldn't drop by the Calderón to see if I had been chosen. My father decided to phone the club to find out. He was the one that gave me the good news, but you would never have thought it.

'You've been selected,' he said, deadpan. 'They've picked six kids and you're one of them. You have to go to Colegio Amorós in the first week of September for another trial to confirm everything.'

It was there, on a pitch very near to where we'd undergone the first trial, that I came across 'professor' Briñas for the second time. He would later play a big role in my development. I did well in the second trial too and at the age of eleven I formally signed up for Atlético Madrid's youth team at what's known in Spain as the *alevín* level – Under-12s. My first coach was a man by the name of Manolo Rangel.

In September 1995 I made a huge leap: from playing football in my local neighbourhood of Fuenlabrada for Rayo 13 to travelling to Belgium for an international tournament with Atlético Madrid. I was nervous just going with my mum to buy a wash bag for the trip to Brussels. I was used to leaving the training pitch covered in mud and going home to shower. At Atlético things were much more organised. Everything had changed. Going to that tournament was my first-ever game away from home. I'd never travelled anywhere without my parents before and I'd never been abroad either. Yet here I was catching a plane, taking days off from school and playing football against Anderlecht, Feyenoord and Borussia

Dortmund. When we got back, three weeks' training awaited us on the pitches at Orcasitas in southern Madrid, in the neighbourhood of Usera, and soon there were matches every Saturday. I was living a dream.

Well before joining Atlético Madrid, even before that cold afternoon at the Calderón, I had already decided that red and white were my colours. When you're a kid you tend to follow your parents; you go to games with them and have an affinity for their team. Or you get dragged along by the family's footballing faith. If your parents don't have a team, choosing can be hard – unless you find an idol to help you make up your mind, a star player to follow. Until I was seven, I wasn't sure who my team should be. At school, almost everyone was a Real Madrid fan and that was the thing that my grandfather Eulalio most complained about. He explained to me, patiently and simply, what being an *atlético* was all about. He told me about the special feeling that surrounds the club. He didn't tell me about players; what he told me about was what it means to wear the Atlético Madrid badge on your chest, with the bear and the strawberry tree emblem that symbolises the city. He told me about the values the club represents and always had done over 100 years of history: hard-work, humility, sacrifice, and overcoming adversity; about resistance to Real Madrid, the city's football giants …

Atlético are a big club too – but for different reasons. Atlético Madrid represent a permanent battle against the odds; being an *atlético* means never giving in, always fighting to the last. Atlético Madrid are on their own, fighting against the establishment, doing it the hard way. It is the people against the power. That's why my grandfather will always be an *atlético*. That's why I will be too.

We Atlético fans are aware that there is a huge difference between the two big clubs in Madrid. Real Madrid have been named the twentieth century's best club and living in the shadow of them is extremely hard. But I am proud of supporting Atlético. It's hard because you don't have constant success to cheer but that's the path I've chosen. I have never been struck by doubts. I've always been committed. Our successes are ours and ours alone; we have done it all on our own. That makes them more real.

I didn't care about being surrounded by Real Madrid fans at school. Back then, two of us bucked the trend: it was me and one Espanyol fan up against 28 Madridistas. If we lost, so what? There'd be another game along soon and we'd win that one. It wasn't only Real Madrid: I also ignored the influence of my father and turned my back on Deportivo de La Coruña. Those were the years of SuperDepor, when Deportivo were the most important team in Galicia and a real sensation in Spain, with Arsenio Iglesias as coach and players like the Brazilians Bebeto and Mauro Silva, plus Liaño, Fran, Manjarín, Aldana, and Djukic. I was given a Deportivo kit when I was nine but I already knew my destiny was red and white, not blue and white.

My first year at the club was wonderful. Not only did the Atlético *alevín* team that I was playing in enjoy a lot of success, the first team did too. Under Radomir

Antić, they achieved an historic double: they won the Copa del Rey, the Spanish equivalent of the FA Cup, by defeating Barcelona and then they won the league after beating Albacete in the Calderón on the final day of the season. All of the club's youth team players had been given a ticket for the match and sat together in the stadium. My father parked the car about twenty minutes away – as anyone who's been there knows, getting any closer to the Calderón by car is impossible – and the walk to the ground was emotional. Everyone was so excited. There was such hope in the air as you passed stalls selling scarves and shirts, drinks and nuts, sweets and crisps. You could feel that it was going to be special.

It's not easy to make the first team. Of those kids who started out with me at Atlético only Manu del Moral, now at Getafe; Molinaro, who plays for Mallorca, and Sporting Gijón's Raúl Cámara are playing in the first division. As time goes by, you realise how important it is to have a coach who really trusts in the young players coming through and has the nerve to call on them if you are going to have any

Playing against Zidane was a unique experience. He was an extraordinary and inimitable footballer; everything he did was special.

chance of making it. It helps to have the media on your side too, ready to support you when you're first starting out and you don't immediately get the benefit of the doubt like a big-name player would. The pressure that surrounds a club means that it is very hard for youth team players to be given the time to play and settle in. The best thing for clubs to do is sign key players for the first team and use the kids coming through to help make up the squad. The truth is, though, that clubs tend to turn to home-grown talents in times of need and pressure, when things are going badly. It would be better to turn to youth team players when things are going well and give them the chance to settle in but that is rare. If things are going well, there is little need to call up a youth-teamer. If Atlético Madrid hadn't been in the second division, I am sure it would have taken longer for me to get a chance.

There are some very talented kids coming through in England, although I think they would be more successful with a strong reserve league. At Liverpool we have two perfect examples: Steven Gerrard and Jamie Carragher have progressed all the way through the club and played for the English national side. There are others too: Wayne Rooney, who started at Everton, Giggs and Beckham at Manchester United and John Terry at Chelsea. The biggest clubs are investing more and more in their academies because they know that there is one thing money can't buy: the spirit and commitment of those players who have been at the club ever since they were kids.

I was never fortunate enough to play with my idol, Kiko. When I came on against Albacete it was in place of him. Never having played a minute with him is a huge disappointment.

III
My debut

It all happened in a flash,
so fast I hardly noticed.
I had made my professional debut.
My first minutes as an Atlético Madrid
player shot by on a warm
spring morning in May.
At the age of seventeen years,
two months and seven days,
my dream became a reality.

Almost seven years after that trial at Parque de las Cruces, I took my first steps as a player at the Vicente Calderón, running on to play the final 26 minutes of Atlético versus Leganés in the Second Division – the division we had been relegated to the previous summer and the division we were trying to escape in the final, frantic weeks of the 2000–01 season.

After the emotion of pulling on that red and white shirt with the No. 35 on the back, I showered, put my Atlético tracksuit back on and gave my first-ever press conference in the press room under the stand at the Calderón. My head still in the clouds, I left the stadium. Alone, I strolled out of gate 6 and looked around for my dad standing amongst the fans who always waited by the players' entrance. It was about 3pm and my stomach was rumbling: I was starving. A few metres away, my parents and my brother and sister were waiting for me by the car. Together we went to eat at a restaurant in a shopping centre in the south of the city, not far from Fuenlabrada where we lived. A family lunch full of hope – what better way to celebrate my debut? I look back on it now and I see myself eating, relaxed, still wearing my Atlético tracksuit. I had just walked away from the Calderón having played my first-ever game but I remember the tranquillity, the calmness of it all.

No one recognised me. I wasn't the fans' favourite; I was just another anonymous kid from the youth team hoping that one day I could make it at Atlético.

It was a quiet Sunday afternoon: phone on silent, a siesta and an evening stroll with the same kids from the neighbourhood as always. The same park, the same people, and the same scenery brought me back down to earth. I had been floating since I had taken a call from Paulo Futre; the Portuguese playmaker, who'd been at Porto, Atlético Madrid, Benfica and Milan, had been our sporting director for the previous six months. It was his job to get us back into the First Division. Futre, who spoke a mix of Portuguese and Spanish every bit as quick as he had been on the pitch, phoned me one Monday to explain what the club's plans were for the 2002–03 season. Promotion was on the horizon and Paulo explained that on Wednesday he wanted me to start training with the first team to gain experience for the future. He also wanted me to join the first team for pre-season training during the summer and then return to the B team to play in Spain's Second Division B.

At first I wasn't keen on the idea. I had gone three successive summers without a break and I was already looking forward to the following week, when I was due to go to Galicia and spend a few days with my grandparents and then head to the beach

with my friends. The day after the conversation with Paulo, the first team had the day off and I was unable to relax. Eventually, the time passed and the big day arrived.

My dad accompanied me to Atlético's training ground in Majadahonda, fifteen kilometres north-west of Madrid – not least because I wasn't yet old enough to drive. I was nervous as I headed towards the first-team dressing room, going down the stairs with my head bowed and in silence. It was still early but it was already hot. Just as I was about to go into the dressing room I saw Fernando, a goalkeeper from the same youth team as me. He had been called up to join in the session led by Carlos García Cantarero, the coach who had been in charge of the first team for the previous four weeks. Having seen 'Ferdy', I felt a little more relaxed as we walked slowly, cautiously, into that dressing room. Ramón, one of the kit men, was there to greet us. 'Come on, lads,' he said, 'this is Atléti!' We didn't know what to do or where to go, so he showed us where to change and gave us the kit. There was still an hour to go before the session started.

I began my first-ever training session with the Atlético first team nervously and barely said a word. We were preparing for the weekend's game against Leganés and as I looked around I saw Kiko Narváez, my boyhood idol and the man I had always tried to emulate, and a host of other familiar faces: Toni Muñoz, Juanma López, Santi Denia, and Roberto Fresnedoso, all of whom had been part of the double winning side, and Carlos Aguilera, one of the club's historic greats. I glanced nervously at them all. The coach welcomed me and so did the club captains, Muñoz, López and Kiko. Then I trained, a novice determined to take my chance. Once it was over and I was back in the dressing room, I felt more relaxed. It helped that José Juan Luque, Iván Amaya and Sergio Sanchez – who, like me, were represented by Bahía Internacional – never left me alone for a second. They kept an eye out for me and the jokes flying round helped me to settle too. Then came the good news when Cantarero said: 'Come back tomorrow.'

Things moved so fast that I hardly had time to do anything, not even to think about what was happening. I hadn't stopped since Spain had won the Under-16 European Championships in England. The week after that, Iñaki Sáez called me up to the Spanish Under-19s to play against Portugal for the second leg following a 1–1 draw in the first match. I scored and so did Oscar González, who currently plays for

Olympiakos in Greece, and we won 2–0. We travelled back to Spain but I hardly had time to unpack before I was off again, this time to Seville with the Atlético youth team for the Copa de España. And that was immediately followed by the call from Futre … All that in barely two weeks. And then my name was on the list for the first-team squad; two amazing weeks might even end with me playing at the Vicente Calderón.

After four training sessions, García Cantarero included me in the squad to face Leganés. When the final session finished Antonio Llarandi, one of the kit men, asked me if I wanted a lift home with him as we both lived in Fuenlabrada, which really helped. It made it easier for me when it came to joining up with the rest of the squad in our pre-match hotel and of course it allowed my dad to have a day off from driving me everywhere. And so I arrived at the Calderón with Antonio, from where the team bus took us to the city-centre hotel where we spent the night – the night before my debut.

My mind went back a fortnight to when the Atlético fans had paid homage to Sergio Torres and me for having been part of the Spain squad that became European Under-16 champions in Sheffield. We had been invited to take the honorary kick-off at the Calderón for Atléti's match with Sevilla before watching the game from the stands. That was only recently but already it felt like it belonged to the past. My debut with the first team was drawing closer.

Atlético's club delegate Carlos Peña put me in a room with David Cubillo, another youth teamer making his way. 'Cubi' had made his debut that season in the first few months of the campaign. He was the perfect room-mate: someone who had gone through the same process that I was now going through. And yet, incredible though it may seem, I was relaxed and far from nervous. I didn't feel the weight of responsibility upon me; that was the captain's duty, not mine. I also knew that I would be sitting on the bench. And even the kick-off time helped: I was used to playing at midday. It was a miracle to be there amongst the chosen ones but I was fairly relaxed and, believe it or not, I slept like a log. It was a reward for me to even be there, so there were no nerves and no anxiety to keep me awake. Nothing worried me.

I took my seat in the dugout and the fans gave me my first round of applause as an Atlético player. I felt like one of them, only I was wearing my kit. Another *atlético* from the youth team, another kid coming through – just as Cubillo, López, Zahínos and Carlos Aguilera had done that very season. It sounded good to me. The fans had given me the thumbs-up. In the meantime, the game went on around me: 0–0 at half-time. At the start of the second half, Cantarero sent me to warm up. As I ran along the touchline, the fans gave me another warm ovation, even bigger this time than before the match. As I stretched, Atléti piled forward but couldn't get the goal. Ten minutes passed and the coach called me over; it was time to go on. But just as I was getting ready Luque scored to make it 1–0 and the coach changed his mind and sent me back along the touchline to continue the warm up.

As I headed along the touchline towards the south end, the fans were celebrating the goal but that didn't stop one or two of them having a go at the coach for taking so long to send me on. A few minutes later – I'm not sure how many it actually was but it felt like an age – he called me over again. This time there was no turning back. This time I really was going on. I was about to make my bow as an Atlético Madrid player.

A strange sensation washed over me as I embraced the goalscorer and ran on in his place. I looked up at the stadium, and I remember thinking how enormous it was. I looked up and down the stands where I had stood as a fan and thought: 'Here I am, where I always dreamed of being.'

But there was no time for me to gaze around and think or for aimless daydreaming. I soon discovered that the pace and intensity of first-team football was far greater than anything I had been used to with the youth team. I called for the ball, I showed for it, but my team-mates didn't find me. Not, that is, until Juan Gómez made a twenty yard run and played it in to me. It was my first touch. I didn't get very involved in the game because I was an unknown, even for my own team-mates. The two most significant moments were when I controlled the ball with my back to goal and won a free-kick, and a lob that went much higher than

I had intended. Atlético won 1–0 but I have never really felt part of that victory. Maybe I hadn't yet got it into my head that I was no longer just another fan.

I was included in the squad for the next match against Albacete six days later, too. It wasn't a huge surprise. I half expected to be included in the trip to La Mancha in central Spain because the team had picked up a lot of cards against Leganés and there were a number of players suspended. And yet at the same time I half expected to be told I could go off on holiday and switch off, not worry about the first team. The match was another do or die encounter in the battle for promotion. Atlético had won three and drawn one since Cantarero had taken over and there were three weeks left until the end of the season. I started on the bench again and came on in place of Kiko.

Looking back with the benefit of hindsight, it is hugely disappointing that I never got the chance to actually play with my idol. I never set foot on the pitch at the same time as him and never played a single minute alongside him, although at least I can say I shared a dressing room with him and was his team-mate for a short period of time. When I went on there were seventeen minutes left and I was lucky enough to score in front of plenty of *rojiblancos*: the stands at the Carlos Belmonte stadium in Albacete were packed with Atléti fans. Ivan Amaya's cross forced me to make a sideways run to throw off the defender and reach the ball. I headed it back across goal, past Valbuena, onto the post and into the net.

The victory gave us a genuine chance of promotion back to the first division with two weeks to go. We were fighting it out with Betis and Tenerife, whose coach was a certain Rafa Benítez. Everything changed for me with that goal. Suddenly, I was the star. I was surrounded by journalists and photographers. I felt like the lead role in a film until one of my team-mates, Hernández, rescued me from the pack. The atmosphere in the dressing room was fantastic and Kiko, who had been captain that day, came up to me and handed me the armband. 'One day you'll wear it on the pitch,' he said. 'Today, you've earned the right to wear it off the pitch.' It's a memento I will keep forever and one that takes pride of place in my house in Madrid.

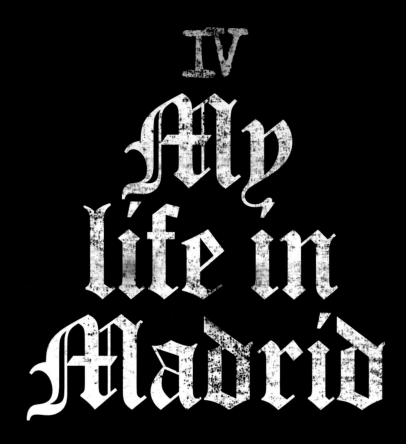

IV
My life in Madrid

A journalist once asked for an interview with me which involved taking photographs in the very centre of Madrid. Atlético Madrid's press officer at the time said yes and called me over one day after training. 'We're going to do an interview and some photos in the Plaza Mayor and the Puerta del Sol,' he told me. The Plaza Mayor and the Puerta del Sol are two of the most emblematic, and busiest, squares in the heart of Madrid.

'Are you mad?' I asked. 'It'll be fine,' he replied, 'no one knows who you are.'

He wasn't wrong. It was Christmas 2001, I was seventeen and had been in the Atlético first team for barely six months. I was virtually anonymous and we did the shoot alongside the stalls that set up for Christmas in the Plaza Mayor, under the famous clock in the Puerta del Sol and with my arms around the statue of the bear and the strawberry bush – the city's emblem and the centrepiece of Atlético's shield. We then rounded off the day with a squid sandwich, typical of the centre of old Madrid. And there hadn't been the slightest hassle.

A goal against Deportivo de La Coruña and then another one against FC Barcelona changed my life. I went from being just another anonymous kid to being recognised by almost everyone.

Fame comes so quickly and there is nothing you can do about it. It creeps up on you and before you know it you're engulfed by it; suddenly, you're thrust into the public eye.

Madrid's waxwork museum wanted me to join the other illustrious sportsmen and women in their hall of fame. This is the day of the unveiling.

A year after that Christmas stroll round Madrid, my name crossed borders. In four matches, I went from a virtual unknown to a player people were talking about. The goal I put past Deportivo goalkeeper José Molina, having flicked the ball over the head of Nourredine Naybet, and another strike, this time against Barcelona, having cut inside Frank De Boer and beaten Roberto Bonano with the outside of my boot, made everyone sit up and take notice. The club had to put the brakes on. Between those two matches, we faced Real Madrid and the press department had over forty requests for interviews with me. I was no longer going step by step; now I seemed to be taking off. People started to recognise me and the pressure grew. It was more and more common for me to appear on the cover of the papers and doing normal things became more difficult. Just going to eat, to the cinema, a concert or even out for a coffee became a trial. Nothing would ever be the same again.

My independence had vanished. That became clear to me during the autumn of 2004. Just after the summer holidays, I got a letter telling me that Madrid's waxwork museum was going to make a model of me. I couldn't understand why they wanted to put me in there alongside other figures from Spanish sport. After the measurements were done, the model was finished in October and I went along to its unveiling. I was the first Atlético player to be immortalised there. Alongside 'me' were Zidane and Raúl as well as a number of other sportsmen and women, like Ángel Nieto, thirteen times motorcycle world champion, Miguel Indurain, five-times winner of the Tour de France, Carlos Sainz, twice world rally champion, and Arantxa Sánchez Vicario, one of the greatest Spanish tennis players ever. There I was, a waxwork in Atlético's centenary kit with a ball in my right hand, signed by my team-mates.

Two months later, a proposal arrived from the Madrid city council. I was asked to inaugurate the city's Christmas celebrations from the balcony of the town hall in the Plaza de la Villa, accompanied by the mayor of Madrid, Alberto Ruiz-Gallardón. It was my duty to turn on the lights and read the *pregón* – the announcement that officially opens the Christmas period.

I was becoming overrun by events, requests and my increasing fame. So much so that my girlfriend Olalla had to start buying my clothes for me: I could only turn up at the shops if I went early in the morning on a weekday. Any other time of day was impossible; I couldn't do something as simple as duck into a fitting room and try something on. It got to the stage that if we wanted to go to the cinema we would turn up in the dark after the film had already started so that no one would see me. We started doing that after one occasion when people had seen me go in or had noticed me sitting alongside them. At the end, loads of mobile phone messages later, there was a huge crowd of people waiting by the doors for me to come out. When I mentioned it to my team-mates in the Spain squad, the ones who played in England told that it would never happen over there.

You do get used to it and you do learn to live with fame, though. Two more events also shot me into the public eye. The first happened when I made my debut for Spain in a friendly against Portugal on 6 September 2003; the second started off as a joke but ended up becoming a big deal and making me even more

recognisable. I was eating with my friend Dani Martín, lead singer of the band El Canto del Loco, and he asked me to appear in a video alongside the actress Natalia Verbeke. It was great fun. Now when I see a video on the television I have some idea of what went into it. Not even half of what you do ends up in the video; we did so much filming and in the end it seemed so short. I was there until late one night and Dani didn't finish until dawn. There must have been a thousand takes, but I was delighted with the final product. The same thing happened when another Spanish group, Café Quijano, came to Las Rozas to play us the song they had written to accompany the Spanish national team at Euro 2004. I was the first to leap on the stage and grab a guitar. And I can't play a single note.

That wasn't the only time Dani has got me into trouble. I must confess, I went red when he called me up onto the stage during one of their concerts in Fuenlabrada. But the worst was what happened to us in a shopping centre in northern Madrid one day. I don't even go to shopping centres often but one day I went with him to a shop that a friend of his owned. I had no idea what going shopping with a pop star was like but I soon found out. In a flash, we were surrounded by people. We couldn't even get out of the shop. In the end, the shop assistant had to shut the place and call in security to clear people out while we escaped through the back door.

They say you know you're famous when you end up on *Spitting Image*, and that happened to me too when Canal Plus's *Noticias del Guiñol* made a Fernando Torres puppet. I also went on one of Spain's most successful comedy shows, a programme called *7 Vidas*. I played myself in a scene with two fantastic actors, Gonzalo de Castro and Santi Rodríguez. The episode was called 'My Worst Friend's Wedding' and although I felt out of place and very nervous, it was wonderful to be able to go on my favourite show.

As I got more famous, my world got smaller and smaller. I had breakfast at the same cafeteria every morning, alongside a petrol station where a number of my Atlético team-mates met. We then switched and started going somewhere else – a lovely Argentinian patisserie right by the club's training ground. After work, we would stop at a bar for a soft drink near my house and then I'd go home

to rest, and every now and again I'd pop into Madrid for a hamburger, just to make a change from the normal footballer's diet and my usual routine.

What we did with our spare time changed from week to week. We'd flip from tenpin bowling virtually every day to endless games on the PlayStation. If the weather was good, I'd go round the heath near my parents' house on the quad bike that the Spanish Football Federation gave each of the players for qualifying for Euro 2004 in Portugal. Or I'd set up a kickabout with my mates on a tiny 20 x 8 metre pitch in my parents' garden. We called it the Flori Stadium after my mum, who's the one that has to put up with us. Sometimes we'd play away, though, and arrange a kickabout in my neighbourhood and play against the kids there. They were great matches.

Life in Liverpool is more relaxed than in Madrid. I get the kind of space that I was denied in the city of my birth.

'Whatever you do, fame means you end up retreating into ever smaller spaces with your closest friends, loyal people you can trust. When you think about it, you realise you can better control your life from those places that have always been yours. What's the point of living in a big city if you can't enjoy it?'

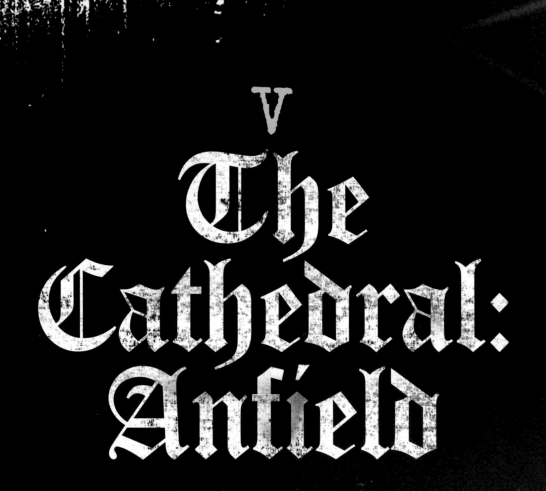

V
The Cathedral: Anfield

'There are two great teams in Liverpool: Liverpool and Liverpool reserves.'

It was Michael Robinson who quoted Bill Shankly's famous remark to me, reciting the words of the manager whose footballing philosophy revolutionised Liverpool Football Club and changed its history forever. Michael, a former Liverpool player and now a commentator on Spanish television, had become my chaperone for the day as we went round the Anfield museum together for a TV documentary. I had been living in the city for six months but I hadn't yet found the time to see one of the jewels in the Reds' crown, although I had been able to take a tour of the stadium with some friends who'd come out from Spain to visit me.

I was struck by the special recognition reserved for the achievements of former players, the men who made the club great. That cold February morning in 2008 Michael explained to me how much Kenny Dalglish Corner means to fans – the area set aside for the European Cups Liverpool so brilliantly won. He also explained the significance of the memorials erected in memory of those fans who so brutally lost their lives at Hillsborough and the mosaics produced in honour of the those who, with their love, fidelity and pride helped to carry Liverpool's name beyond the city gates. If there is one thing that has really stood out for me since I've been in England, it's the huge human tide of Liverpool fans. It's incredible. I have never seen a single Liverpool fan criticise a player, even when the team has lost. Every player dreams of fans like that; here at Anfield, we've got them.

Six months had passed since that special day at Anfield in July 2007 when my signing was announced to the press. An afternoon's rain had given way to bright sunshine on Merseyside. I didn't know the drill, so Benítez explained what would happen during my presentation. 'It's not like it is in Spain,' he said. 'Normally, we unveil our players quietly, almost privately, at Melwood. But because you cost so much, we're going to have to open Anfield.' I had seen Liverpool players presented before. I remembered Luis García and Xabi Alonso's first day. I knew that I wouldn't have to go out in full kit, boots and all, and do kick-ups on the pitch so that photographers could capture the moment and send the image round the world, as happens in Spain. I seemed to remember Luis and Xabi simply posing in tracksuits, holding Liverpool scarves, and I was wearing a suit and smart shoes, ready for my press conference. But soon I found myself in a small room slipping off my jacket, shirt and tie and pulling on the red shirt of Liverpool. It was the first time I'd worn the shirt of any other club apart from Atlético. I looked at myself in the mirror: there I was in red. I was still wearing No. 9 but I was transformed.

I looked down; my trousers and shoes hadn't changed. Wearing a football shirt and smart trousers and shoes, looking a bit strange, I walked down the corridor towards the mythical tunnel that leads to the Anfield pitch. Rafa stopped in front of the 'This is Anfield' sign. 'Shankly put that here so that everyone knew exactly where they were,' he said. 'You'll hear Shankly's name a lot at this club.' He was right. The previous night I'd started reading the books and watching the DVDs on Liverpool's history that I'd been given to help me learn about the club. Shankly, Paisley, Dalglish … just some of the names I had managed to commit to memory in the last few frenetic days. And, as we climbed the stairs, Shankly popped up again as Benítez told me a story about him and Kevin Keegan.

We sat in the stands at Anfield, flashes going off all around us. I was wearing a short-sleeved shirt and I felt a chill. I thought to myself: 'And it's supposed to be July!' I turned to Rafa and said: 'Wow, it's cold!' 'Cold? Here? It's never cold here,' he replied with a grin. I looked up and saw the exact image of what I had always imagined an English stadium to be: small, tight, just 45,000 seats, with the stands right up against the pitch, old but warm – a ground with feeling. What a noise this place must make! It made me realise how important the history of the club is, the traditions that are passed on by fans, the flags and anthems and banners – the whole match-day ritual, which is seeped in the club's history. Every little detail matters, unlike in Spain where clubs' identities are being lost – some newer generations of fans simply don't know how to pass on the traditions and identities of their clubs and that makes them feel uncomfortable.

From the stands, we carried on down the stairs, stopping at the dugouts en route. I hardly even realised they were there because they're so set-back, just normal seats embedded in amongst the fans in the Main Stand. 'I don't want to see you here again,' Benítez warned. Understood, boss. It wasn't until the third game of the season that I even realised where the technical area was marked out, it was so small.

After the photos had been taken, it was time for me to say my first public words as a Liverpool player. First, though, I asked one of the members of staff to look after my first Liverpool shirt for me so that I could take it home with me later. No sooner were the words out of my mouth than Benítez pointed out that players' shirts are normally donated to charity after their presentation. Because they're so

special, being the first shirt a player has ever worn, they normally raise a lot of money. No problem. My shirt was donated to a cancer charity that auctioned it off. An Irish businessman got it in return for £4,900.

With the coach acting as translator, the club's press officer explained how the press conference would work. It would be divided into four parts for four different sets of journalists. In Spain, you do one press conference for all of the media together and that's it. I caught the eye of one of the Spaniards accompanying me; he just shrugged and said: 'Welcome to England!' The first stop was in front of the television cameras, and I sat down alongside a nice guy called Phil, the translator.

Before I spoke to the media, Rafa joked about the fact that I had spoken to the Madrid media that very morning at the Vicente Calderón. 'You told them that Atlético Madrid will always be in your heart,' he smiled. 'So, think carefully about what you're going to say now. You might have to tell them you've got a very big heart – one with room for both clubs.'

What I told them was something along the lines of: 'I've signed for a huge club, a team of champions, one of the biggest clubs in the world. I hope I can contribute to their success and become a champion myself.'

The media merry-go-round continued with Phil and Ian Cotton, the club's press officer, permanently by my side: a general press conference, radio, daily

The Hillsborough Memorial in honour of those who died in the tragedy touches me in a special way. It's wonderful how our fans keep the memory alive – they will never forget.

newspapers and then the Sundays. Just when I thought I had finally finished, Phil took me into another room. With a look of fear in his eyes, he said: 'Now, you've got to talk to Liverpool TV and the club's official website.' Well, seeing as we're here ... There wasn't a minute to think or relax and I immediately realised that things were going to be very different in England. There was so much to get used to.

When I flew to Liverpool for the second time in two days, I still wasn't aware that my life was changing by the minute. So much was happening that I needed to take a step back and pause for a moment but there just wasn't a chance to do so. On the way to the presentation that afternoon we had been waiting at passport control at Liverpool airport when a group of fans recognised me. They gave me an amazing ovation and I began signing autographs but I couldn't hang about because we had to get through passport control. There was a car waiting to take us to Anfield. As I was on my way there, I got a call from my childhood hero Kiko Narváez, the former Atlético Madrid player and one of the stars of their double-winning team, who'd rung to wish me luck. He had listened to what I said during the press conference at the Calderón in the morning and he told me that he thought I'd made the right decision. The call over, there was silence in the car, broken only by the sound of the engine, and I watched distractedly out the window as the city went by. Just as we were going past Goodison Park, the man Liverpool had asked to look after me, Owen, said something. Jorge Lera, a friend of mine from Bahía Internacional, translated for me as he pointed up at the ground: 'He says: "I hope you score loads of goals."'

We went into Anfield through the Memorial Gate and Jorge translated as Owen explained what happened at Hillsborough in 1989, when so many Liverpool fans died. It was a tragedy provoked by negligence and one for which there still hasn't been an explanation. Rick Parry, Liverpool's chief executive, and Rafa Benítez were waiting for us in the room where the managers' families wait on match day. The room where I was to sign my contract with Liverpool. Margarita Garay, one of my representatives at Bahía, had just finished making some minor alterations to a couple of clauses when I walked in. I took short steps, glancing at the pictures on the walls, looking at the other people in the room. I took no notice of the food that had been laid on for me. Who could eat at a moment like that? I was handed a pen and I signed the contract that bound me to Liverpool for six years. Benítez congratulated me in typical style: 'You've got to get to the gym. You're too thin to play in England.'

It took a few months for me to get to know every corner of the stadium. One of the most emblematic is the dressing room. On a match day you go in through the players' entrance to the sound of the fans singing and chanting alongside the team bus. You go along a narrow corridor, turn right and come to a room that has not changed in a hundred years. It's a small room with benches, pegs on the walls, two treatment tables and a table in the middle covered with bandages and strappings and other equipment. The players take up half the room, the coaches and backroom staff the other, but this year the staff have taken to using an old storeroom to try to gain a little space. Before every game, Steven Gerrard or Dirk Kuyt take charge of the music, just as Sergio Ramos does with the Spanish national team.

You look around and think it's a small space for so many people, but tradition dictates. There's no room for luxury at Liverpool. As Gerrard told Benítez and Robbie Fowler told Gerard Houllier: 'This is where Liverpool players have always changed – the same Liverpool players who have won countless titles. We're no bigger than they are.'

The dressing room is an extension of the pitch and the rest of the ground. Anfield is not a modern mega-stadium but the history that surrounds it is far more important.

On your way out to the pitch, you can't get lost: the tunnel only goes one way, towards the greatest of stages. You really notice the silence as you make your way there. I think the opposition know that something special is going to happen and they're quiet too, trying to take in the moment. As you reach a small opening at the top of the stairs, a kind of improvised waiting room, the silence is broken by players geeing each other up and the sound of 'You'll Never Walk Alone' coming from outside. It's a song that sets your heart racing and gets the adrenaline pumping, ready for the battle that's about to begin.

When I signed for Liverpool on that summer evening, I asked the club to get me twenty shirts with my name and number on so that I could take them back to Spain with me and give them to my friends. It had been such a hectic day that I'd completely forgotten all about them until I was at John Lennon Airport and I heard a shout from Owen, standing there with a bag in each hand. 'Fernando,' he called out, 'your shirts'.

VI

The men who made Liverpool great

'Here, you'll enjoy these.
They'll help you learn something
about the history of this club and
what makes Liverpool great.'

I still remember Owen Brown's words as he handed me two DVDs and two books on Liverpool. Owen is one of the employees at Liverpool and he looked after me as I took my first steps in the city. There were still a few hours to go until I had my medical just before completing my transfer to the Reds, but he already wanted me to familiarise myself with the history of the club since 1892. The first thing that struck me was that Liverpool FC was founded on 15 March, just five days before my birthday; the second was that it all happened because Everton couldn't pay the rent at Anfield.

My first encounter with Liverpool's legends came courtesy of the Spanish journalist Guillem Balagué. He got me and Kenny Dalglish – King Kenny – together for an article for *The Times* newspaper. First, though, I want to talk about a fantastic meal that the former Liverpool player and European Cup winner Michael Robinson organised. He brought together Liverpool players past and present for *Informe Robinson* – the programme that he directs and presents on Canal Plus television in Spain. The meal took place in a restaurant in the heart of Liverpool: four legends from the Liverpool side of the late 1970s and early 1980s, and three representatives of the current 'Spanish Liverpool' team – Dalglish, Graeme Souness, Robinson himself and Sammy Lee, who at that stage wasn't yet part of the coaching staff, plus Pepe Reina, Álvaro Arbeloa (who has since joined Real Madrid) and myself. Xabi Alonso couldn't make it on that cold night in February, while Albert Riera hadn't yet joined the squad.

After we had been introduced to each other, Souness led the conversation. An elegant, charismatic Scotsman, captain of the team that won the European Cup in Rome in 1984, he was a real leader. Halfway through the speech made by a Uefa dignitary after Liverpool had won the 1984 final on penalties, Souness decided he

had heard enough and quickly pulled the cup from his hands to lift it into the sky because Roma's fans had already started leaving. 'I wanted them to see us celebrating,' he said. Sitting there, his character shone through as he talked; you could imagine him as a leader, a captain. But the star was sitting next to him. 'The fans declared Dalglish the greatest player in the club's history,' Souness said. 'They called him the Dog's Bollocks – as good as it gets.'

The four of them were very complimentary towards me. Kenny said that I was Liverpool's best summer signing. Sammy likened me to none other than Ian Rush, the highest goalscorer in the club's history. I listened carefully to everything they said – men who had won it all.

One of the talking points was Rafa Benítez's rotation policy. Souness took no prisoners. 'I'd like to see some of the old Liverpool philosophy. When you have a great group of players, let them express themselves, let them play, let them complement each other,' he insisted.

'Rotation is a mystery. No one knows why Liverpool's best players don't play every game. I would like them to know they're the best, to feel it.'
—Graeme Souness

'I don't think the game is any more demanding than it was when we played, when you take into consideration the fact that players these days look after themselves much better than we did in terms of physical preparation, nutrition, hydration, alcohol … I never felt tired and I played Saturday, Wednesday, Saturday non-stop for fifty weeks a year. It's psychological. You get tired when you lose. Liverpool have rested their best players too often this season.'

Dalglish agreed. 'What's changed is the players' mentality,' he said. 'If you insist on telling a player that he's tired, he'll believe you. If you tell him to play, he'll play. No player ever goes up to the coach and says he's tired, so just get on with it; get out there and play.'

Dalglish also revealed one of the keys to winning six league titles and three European Cups. 'We had great people, a strong dressing room. We were down to earth and also ambitious. We felt like we were nothing special but we always attacked; we always faced up to the opposition. We always went for them,' he said. Dalglish had set it up, now Souness put it away. 'Every year was fantastic because we always won something,' he added. 'If we only won one trophy it was a bad year.'

Over two and a half hours, the three of us listened to stories from the past – Liverpool's current players hanging on every word uttered by Liverpool's legends.

Robinson told us that the team most people rated as the best in the world trained in dirty kit every day, faithful to a tradition that went back to the 1960s.

By the end of the evening, I couldn't thank them enough. It's because of them that we are here today and hopefully one day we'll be sitting on the other side of the table. Souness's response, on behalf of them all, really made us feel special: 'No, thank *you* for listening to a load of nostalgic old men. And remember: they always made us feel like we weren't as good as our predecessors. Our three European Cups weren't as important as the first one the club won.' And with that he wished us good luck.

My first visit to Melwood came just a few minutes after my presentation as a Liverpool player at Anfield – a first glimpse of my new workplace. I went into the dressing room and was shown my locker. Not that it was mine yet: it still belonged to Robbie Fowler and he hadn't emptied it out. The lockers are allocated by shirt number. Mine was No. 9 so I was taking over from a Liverpool legend. I literally took his shirt too: a few months later Liverpool played Cardiff, Robbie's new team, in the Carling Cup and I was told that he wanted to swap shirts with me. I didn't need asking twice. His shirt is a treasure I've kept with pride.

Liverpool's No. 9 has always been special. There was Fowler, of course, and people also told me about Ian Rush, John Aldridge and Roger Hunt – one of the all-time greats. I remembered Robbie's goal celebration against Everton, the one that got him into trouble. I was told about Rush at Anfield and Juventus. About John Aldridge, a clone of Ian Rush. Former players are a key part of every club; they are always there to offer advice and they always want the best for the team. I love talking to them now at Liverpool, just as I did with the greats at Atlético Madrid. Teams are a product of their past and it's important to honour your history. It's the best way to ensure you're on the right path for the future. In Madrid, I used to love talking to Adelardo, who played more games for Atlético than anyone else; to Garate, one of the club's great No. 9s from the 1970s; to Luis Aragonés, a coach and a player for so many years at Atlético; or to Luiz Pereira, the Brazilian defender who's now president of Reserva Atlético. It was thanks to them that the club became great; they are role-models for the players of the future.

There's nothing better than listening to the man who fans consider to be the greatest Liverpool player of all time: Kenny Dalglish. As I said, Guillem wanted to do a report on Liverpool's past and its present. But Kenny and I are not the same: he is the greatest player of all, I was just a new arrival. I had only scored a handful of goals, nowhere near what Kenny had achieved. There was no comparison: I still haven't done anything to even get close to him and I felt a little embarrassed, but Dalglish immediately put me at ease. 'You can only ever be a legend in someone's mind. So long as you never become a legend in your own mind, there's no problem,' he said. 'People want to pigeon-hole you, Fernando; they want to label you, rank you, judge you and compare you to others. But all that really matters is that you are yourself.'

Balagué reminded me that Kenny and I do have things in common: we're both strikers, we're both Pisces, we were both Liverpool's record signing and, he said, we're both capable of turning the Kop into 'a frenzied hive of humanity' … more importantly, Liverpool unites us. As Guillem put it: 'That's what this club is all about. Players come and go, but the shirt and the continuity remain. Torres plays with Jamie Carragher, who played with Robbie Fowler, who played with John Barnes, who played with Ian Rush, who played with Dalglish. And Dalglish played with Emlyn Hughes, who played with Ian St John, who played with Roger Hunt, who played with Ronnie Moran, who played with … Well, you can keep it going all the way back to Malcolm McVean, the man who scored the first goal in Liverpool's history in 1892.'

The other thing we have in common is goals. Dalglish told me that we're the ones who make people's dreams come true. The fans can't play, so they live their dreams through us. Then Kenny revealed something that surprised me: 'I always wanted to go on the Kop, but I never could,' he said. 'The only time I have ever been on the Kop is when the stadium has been empty. It's funny, my son has been there but I haven't. A friend of mine took him and looked after him;

he spent the game with him on the Kop. He lived a dream that I couldn't.' Like Kenny, I've only been on the Kop when it was empty. I would love to think that when I retire it will be impossible for me to watch a game from the Kop too. That would mean I had achieved something great.

Dalglish told me, as he later repeated during that meal with Souness, Lee and Robinson, that the key to Liverpool's success was the harmony within the team. 'No team has ever been successful without a good atmosphere in the dressing room,' he said. 'They don't have to go out for drinks together or be best friends, but having a good group is very important. We had a great dressing room, we were really united. Even now there are six or seven of us that are still close. We play golf, we go out with our wives. It's special. That doesn't happen now, does it? In twenty years time there won't be six of you still round the club.' Who knows? What I do know for sure is that we are all committed to keeping Liverpool great.

During that meeting we talked and talked about football. I talked about the fact that there are games when things don't go for you but that I will never hide. I always want the ball, even if I'm having a bad day. Liverpool's legendary No. 7 said he was the same. 'Of course you want the ball. You have to keep going. As a striker, you miss more chances than you score. The goals aren't what matter most; what matters most are the chances you miss. The more you miss, the closer you are to the next one you're going to score. You have to think like that: if you don't have the courage to develop that kind of attitude you won't make it at this level.'

I'm not the kind of person who watches a lot of football on television; when I do it's because I want to know about other teams, about my opponents. I have to study them and prepare myself properly to face them.

In Dalglish's era, there weren't so many games broadcast on television, so he had to go and watch players, to see what habits the goalkeepers had, what the outstanding qualities of the defences were, to see if he could learn anything. Then, later on, he watched games to see if there was a player he might like to sign. 'But,' Kenny said, 'I don't enjoy it as much as I did when I was a kid.'

I learned so much from my time with Kenny. I really like him. He's a normal person who's very accessible. He says he doesn't feel like a legend but that's exactly what he is. The fact that he has stayed so normal really struck me. I can't be compared to him but I feel proud to have been able to speak to him for so long. It was a real honour for him to have given up his time to talk to me. Meeting Kenny has made me even more hungry for success, even more determined to work hard and maybe, just maybe, see if one day I can compare myself with him.

I'll never forget the last piece of advice he gave me, as we were leaving the restaurant. Just as he went out the door, the greatest player in the history of Liverpool turned to me and said: 'Fernando, Liverpool is a special club with special fans. They love those players who love wearing their shirt. But they're not stupid: they know when players mean it and when they don't; they know when it's just for show – when a player kisses the badge and all that. They love to identify themselves with the players out on the pitch and I think they're going to identify with you very, very easily.'

What an honour.

VII

The captain's armband

'Welcome to Liverpool FC. I'm looking forward to meeting you and training together. Good luck and hopefully we can be successful together.'

Steven Gerrard

I had just landed at the Torrejón de Ardoz airbase outside Madrid after a hectic first day in Liverpool. I turned on my mobile phone, which was packed with unread texts and answerphone messages that I hadn't yet listened to, and started working my way through them. As I was doing so, two new messages arrived. The first was from Steven Gerrard. A few seconds later another turned up, this time from Jamie Carragher. Both were written in English. I tried to read them but in the end had to hand the phone over to Jorge Lera, without whom I would have been sunk during those first few days in England. He translated for me. I'd barely been a Liverpool player for five hours and already the club captains had sent me an unexpected welcome. I turned to the others in the car and said: 'What a nice touch that is.' It was, I thought to myself, a really fantastic gesture.

I've been a captain too. During my last two seasons at Atlético Madrid I was the leader in the dressing room. Before that I had shared the role with Carlos Aguilera, one of the most important players in the history of the club. Only three players have played more games for Atlético: Adelardo Rodríguez, Tomás Reñones and Enrique Collar. But the truth is, I should never have taken on that responsibility so young.

Being captain doesn't just mean wearing the armband. You have to be an example to others and to do that you need experience.

Aguilera was one thing, but I'd never had time to gain that experience. And yet the turnover of players was so fast that by the time I was in my second year I was already one of the players who'd been there the longest. At first, I watched the way

that Carlos Aguilera and Santi Denia led the players but I was only with them for two years; I was only able to learn from them for a short time. It wasn't enough.

Other great players turned up who had much more experience than I did. How could I be expected to lead players like Demetrio Albertini, Diego 'Cholo' Simeone, Demis Nikolaidis, Sergi Barjuan or Leo Franco? I was lucky that they never ceased helping me out in my attempts to be a good captain. So much so that I built a better relationship with the veterans of the team than the players of my own age. I felt I had to take refuge in that group in order to learn and seek advice. I still miss their company, even today. Aguilera was the player who taught me the most, and with the passage of time I am realising even more than I did then that it's vital that people respect your position. Because of the way the squad was at Atlético, I had been promoted too fast and become captain too soon.

Carragher: football mad. Hyypiä: the best team-mate I've ever had.

In Spain, the captain has to be on top of everything, from whether the club have paid the players to how the squad gets on. Every day there's something else to attend to. In England, things are different; there is more structure, more order. Every club has a Player Liaison Officer who looks after the players and allows them to worry about just one thing: playing. That was something I noticed as soon as I arrived in Liverpool. The structure that's set up around the players surprised me; the club takes care of the details and the captains take it upon themselves to ease the pressure on your shoulders, to look after you, and make you feel welcome. They try to help you and lead by example. I really noticed that in training: Gerrard and Carragher, for example, are always the first to do each exercise and their attitude provides a model to follow. Their enthusiasm is contagious; their approach brings the intensity and dedication necessary to everything we do ... if they give everything, then you have no choice but to give everything too. Together, they take responsibility for leading the team, they get on brilliantly and they complement each other perfectly. And although they're the undisputed leaders, no one is jealous of them.

When I arrived, I was told how Gerrard became captain. It happened when Rafa Benítez became coach. At the time, the man everyone looked up to was Sami Hyypiä, who was captain, but Rafa asked the squad, Sami included, who they should have as captain and they decided it was time for Gerrard to take the armband. It didn't matter that he wasn't the longest-serving player; what mattered were his leadership qualities and the fact that the squad looked to him for inspiration. It's not always about having been there for the longest amount of time; it is about who is best equipped to lead the team, with the support of the rest of the squad.

This is a good time to say something about Hyypiä – without doubt the best team-mate I have ever had. Ten out of ten as a player and a person. Everyone loves him. He never complains, he never sulks, you never hear a word out of place from him. I really admire him. In training sessions when we do crossing and finishing exercises, ninety percent of his shots go in. I started calling him the Matador in Spanish; now he calls me it. I told him he had to play his last season as a professional up front because he never misses. But when I said that he just looked at me and said: 'No, you are the Matador.'

Jamie, 'Carra', is football mad. He reminds me a lot of 'Cholo' Simeone because he's always thinking about the game and how he can improve. I'm sure he'll be Liverpool's manager one day. He follows other leagues, too, including La Liga. He is always asking things about Spanish football. When he has time off he watches football all day, every day. On the pitch, he is a strong personality; he is the extension of Benítez, he never lets you relax for a moment, he is always on top of you demanding more. He's very communicative and he quickly wins players over. He treats you the way your effort and behaviour deserves. How does he act with me? I think he likes me.

I admire Steven Gerrard because I know how much pressure he has to live with every day. Everyone's talking about him all the time – in the dressing room, in the bars, in the stadium. From my own experience, I know how difficult it is to keep everyone happy, but the pressure he's under is on a different level to anything I ever had to live with because Liverpool is such a huge club.

When you're captain, you know everyone is talking about you. You can feel it, especially when things go badly. Everything that Gerrard has to face every single day, and the expectations that surround him, make the way he handles the pressure even more impressive. He is always under the microscope and people always expect him to be a leader, to lift the team all on his own. He is an example to everyone who ever finds themselves in that situation. It's incredible what he has to put up with and how much there is going on around him every single day.

I would love to be a captain somewhere some day because I think I've had the best possible role model in Steven Gerrard. At Liverpool, he is irreplaceable. Every big club has a standard bearer, a home-grown talent, someone with a lifelong commitment to the cause. People come and go but he's always there. It's him and ten others. He's everything to his side. That's Steven Gerrard at Liverpool. I can't even begin to imagine the place without him.

He's got it all as a footballer too: personality, consistency, stature, control, power, strength, aggression, intensity, he never goes missing … he can play everywhere and he can play in every way. Wherever you put him, he performs. He scores goals, works hard, he's quick, he's tireless. He's a born leader and the most consistent player in the world. The only thing missing from his CV is the Premier

League title and an international award like the Ballon d'Or or the FIFA World Player and I'm sure he'll win one of those soon. There's no doubt he deserves to. Any coach would want him in their side. It's hard for people to judge just how good he is because he's still playing, but one day he'll be recognised as one of the greatest players in the club's history. And, don't forget, he's Liverpool through and through too: a local lad who came up through the ranks.

That fact makes his achievements all the more impressive to me. For any scouser to get into the Liverpool first team is extremely difficult. The kids in the youth team have it tough because they go straight into the Premier League from the Reserves without having played in the Championship, League One or League Two first. There's no stepping stone. I think they need to compete at a lower level first, rather than just in the Reserves League, because otherwise the leap is too big when it comes to trying to make it in the first team.

Youth teamers learn from the first team players whom they look up to; they get immersed in the values of the clubs and the footballers who represent it over the years. Maybe that's why Steven and Carra haven't had to tell me what Liverpool stands for; I can see it in their game.

Steven doesn't need to scream and shout on the pitch to be a leader. He leads by example, by the way he plays – the way he's had bred into him for years. He is without doubt the greatest player I have ever played with. He has everything. Our captains are symbols of the club: they supported the team as kids, they sweated for the cause for years in the Academy, fighting to make it, they've put up with the pressure of playing for their future with the Reserves, they've made it to the first team and worn the armband at Anfield. I have tried to absorb everything I can from the club and the city, to understand exactly where I am and that's because of them. If there is one thing that inspires me about Carragher and Gerrard, one thing that stands out as the key to the way they play, it is their commitment to the cause.

If there is one thing I would have loved to have been throughout my career it is a one-club man. Just like Gerrard is – he signed an extension that means he will see out his playing days at Liverpool, where it all started for him. Just like Raúl, Carles Puyol, Paolo Maldini and Francesco Totti – men who have given their all for their clubs. They don't know how lucky they are to have been able to triumph with their team. They have done everything, they've won trophies, captained their sides … My progress had stagnated at Atlético Madrid and that – and that alone – forced me to turn my back on my dream. I knew which club I wanted to go to and I made the right choice. Luckily for me, rather than being bitter, those Atlético fans who didn't understand my decision at the time have come to realise why I had to go. The impact is there for all to see: a year after leaving, having played just one season in England, my profile has changed completely. And a year after arriving, my mobile phone still contains two messages that arrived on my first day at Liverpool. The warmest of welcomes from Steven and Carra.

VIII
Living in Liverpool

One of the biggest problems I faced when I first moved to Liverpool was the language barrier. My English was limited to the classes I had taken at school in Fuenlabrada. You think you know a bit of English and that you can get by but when you actually arrive in England you soon realise that you haven't really got a clue.

Despite that problem, my first few weeks were very relaxed. Not all Liverpool fans recognised me; I still wasn't very well known. I could stroll round the city with my girlfriend, round areas like Albert Dock and the city centre, and there were no problems. I walked to restaurants – I still didn't have a car – and I didn't feel like there was the constant hassle that I had been forced to put up with in Madrid. I couldn't believe how much freedom I was getting; I was able to lead a normal life.

That was only at the start, though. Although people are very respectful and things haven't reached the point where they were at in Madrid when I could hardly leave the house, my life in Liverpool has changed since then. Now, it's harder.

Having said that, I really appreciate the way people have treated me in Liverpool. They have always shown a huge amount of respect – so much so that I have had some strange experiences. Like the time a Liverpool fan waited by the entrance to a restaurant for over an hour for me to come out because she didn't want to disturb me while I was eating. She had a Liverpool shirt that she wanted me to sign and didn't want to interrupt me during my meal, even though she had been sitting only two tables away. She finished her meal, left and waited patiently by the door for me to do the same.

When I first arrived, the club found me an apartment near Albert Dock, in Princess Dock. It was the same place I had stayed in when I came over to complete my medical with Liverpool's doctor, Mark Waller. Because I was living right in the centre of the city, I had everything I needed within touching distance. I came back from pre-season in Switzerland to find the fridge completely empty, so I asked the concierge in the building where the nearest supermarket was. He sent me to a

Marks & Spencer in the city centre. I strolled there, still in my Liverpool tracksuit, and thought nothing of it. I did my shopping without getting any hassle from anyone. At first I thought that maybe people had mistaken me for a fan but when I was waiting in the queue to pay, a group of kids turned up, pen in hands, to ask for my autograph.

Liverpool is very different to Fuenlabrada and Majadahonda, the two places I lived in Madrid. In Madrid, you can travel for half an hour without getting very far and think nothing of it; if you travel for half an hour in Liverpool, you're practically in Manchester. I like Liverpool. It's a small, comfortable and welcoming city, where you have everything to hand. Some people say that it lacks this thing or that, but it's fine for my lifestyle.

During the first few weeks, I went everywhere by foot. We'd walk into the city centre and try out various restaurants for lunch or dinner. The idea was to get to know the city as quickly as possible. After all, we were planning to live there for at

Personally, I like the Beatles a lot. Before I ever imagined that I would end up in Liverpool, I listened to their songs. Now I've rediscovered them because listening to them has helped me to pick up the language more quickly. My favourite songs are 'Penny Lane' and 'Yellow Submarine'.

least six years – the length of my contract with Liverpool. We'd go from Princess Dock to Victoria Street or Duke Street to eat in the places we'd had recommended to us. One afternoon, on the way back from having lunch we decided to go shopping. I'd been told about Costco and so we decided to go in and have a look. As we were going through the door, the security guard stopped us. We assumed he was asking for a member's card that we didn't have and so, not being able to explain in English, we just turned and left without a word. The next day I was told that if you're not a member you can't shop there.

As we strolled round the city centre, there was one place we couldn't miss: Matthew Street. I never actually went into The Cavern but I did stroll round the Beatles route. What can I say about the legendary band, a symbol for the city? There's not much I can add, although it did strike me that – despite what you might imagine – people in Liverpool aren't constantly talking about the Beatles and their success. People have an enormous amount of respect and admiration for them, because everyone in Liverpool is conscious of the fact that the Beatles and Liverpool FC have taken the name of their city round the world. Everyone is proud of them … Everton fans permitting, of course.

Personally, I like the Beatles a lot. Before I ever imagined that I would end up in Liverpool, I listened to their songs. Now I've rediscovered them because listening to them has helped me to pick up the language more quickly. My favourite songs are 'Penny Lane' and 'Yellow Submarine'.

I particularly like the city's parks. I love Stanley Park, the one that divides Anfield and Goodison and which I got to know when I went to film the Spanish No. 9 advert for Nike there. I've also been to Chester, and to Formby on the coast where, weather permitting, I like to devour a Flake 99 with raspberry sauce. Sometimes when I go exploring I'm accompanied by staff from Liverpool, especially David Bygroves and Owen Brown. They have been great in helping me to adapt to life in Liverpool, especially at the start. David speaks Spanish and arranged things such as handling all the paperwork you need to deal with when you first turn up in a foreign country. Spending time with Owen has helped too because it forces me to speak English as together we deal with day to day life at Liverpool.

And what day to day task could be more important than driving? The first time I got behind the wheel in Liverpool I committed the same mistake that I imagine lots of people do: I started driving on the wrong side of the road. I made up my mind right from the start that I had to get myself an English car with right-hand drive as soon as possible to help rid myself of the fear of driving in another country. I asked the club to help me buy an English car. I set out from Melwood in it, with Owen driving behind me to help out. I took the first turn full of misplaced confidence – and ended up on the wrong side. Despite that mistake, I think it's easier to get used to than people imagine. In fact, now when I travel back to Spain I think and act as if I was in England. I arrived at Barajas airport and almost got run over by a taxi as soon as I came out of the terminal because I was looking the wrong way when I crossed the road. And when I find myself driving down quiet roads with no markings, I often end up driving the English way, on the left.

I haven't done the tourist routes though. And I'm not one for going to the concerts that are held in the Echo Arena, like the MTV gala. I did, though, make an exception to collect the award for Personality of the Year handed to me by City 96.7. It's the radio station of the moment and the one that I always tune in to when I'm driving because I like the mix of music, entertainment and news. Rafa Benítez and Mikel Arteta were at the ceremony too but, even surrounded by friendly faces, I'm not very comfortable at such big events.

I haven't experienced Liverpool's nightlife. I have been out a couple of times to eat on Tuesdays or Wednesdays after Champions League matches and you can see that there's a lot going on and that people really enjoy themselves. Unlike Spain, where people stay out very late, I'm told that even the biggest partygoers go home earlier in Liverpool. One thing that does surprise me is that no one seems to wear a coat. Everyone is done up and dressed to impress but few of them wrap up warm, even though the temperature can't be much above freezing. One thing I would like to do is watch a game in the pub. Everyone tells me about the passion with which fans follow matches between pints.

The thing that most surprised me came one Christmas when I was told that I had to wear a fancy dress costume for the players' party. I wasn't used to that and I was a bit confused when I was told about it in the dressing room. For a number of reasons, I haven't yet dressed up for one of our Christmas parties but I did go last year and I really stood out … because I was the only one who'd left his costume at home.

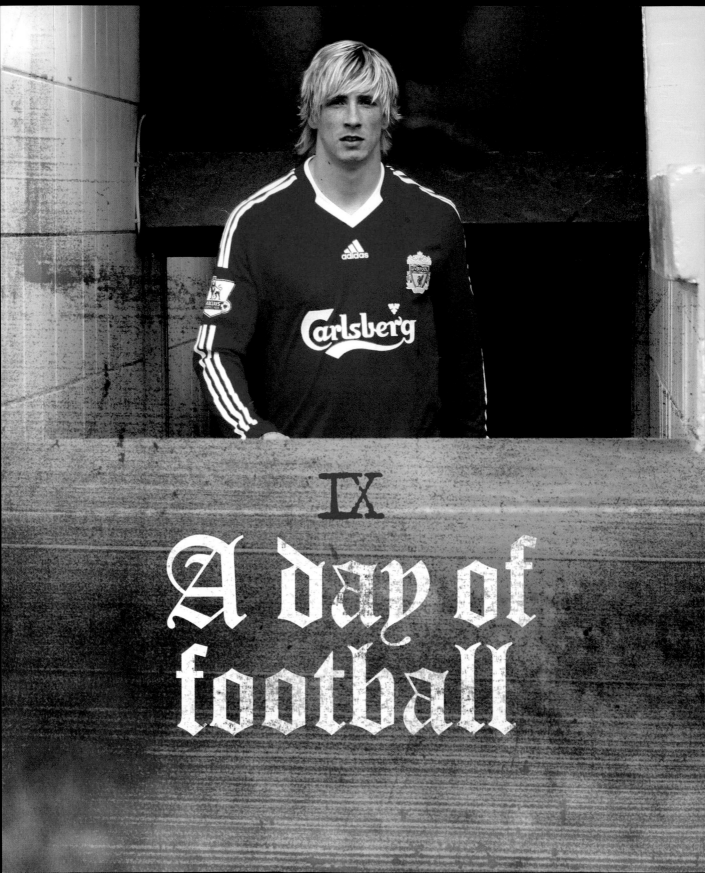

IX

A day of football

I don't like watching myself on television but it is something I do. It's strange but I will only watch my matches again if I am on my own. I don't feel comfortable sharing that moment with other people. Why? Because I am always critical of my own performances and I can be hard on myself.

Looking back on my matches is a tool, a way of improving and learning – it doesn't matter if I played well or if I was dreadful. I try to watch every game with two things in mind: where I went wrong and what I can improve.

I want to use this chapter to tell you what my match-day experience is like and how I prepare for a game in the week building up to it. There are few hard and fast rules in football. The fixture list dictates what you do, but in general if you're playing on Saturday you start getting specific instructions on Thursday and that continues right up to the game.

THE BACKROOM STAFF

That's when the coaching staff start pulling you aside to tell you things one on one. They tell you how the defenders you're going to come up against play, how they organise themselves. For example, I always talk to our goalkeeping coach, Xavi Valero, in the dressing room before every game and together we analyse the opposition's goalkeeper: his strong points, his weak points, if he catches or punches, if he goes to ground early or stays on his feet – a footballing X-ray of the man I have to beat. Because we always talk just before the game, I go out onto the pitch with the information still fresh in my mind.

Dave is another member of Rafa Benítez's team. He's in charge of the video archive. He has every game on DVD and he often shows us a few examples of the opposition's defence in action; he tries to show us where they might be vulnerable and where we can gain an advantage. Sometimes, I'll ask Dave for a specific game and go over it a number of times if I think it will help me understand the way the other team defends and visualise the way they organise themselves.

Football theory is fine, and it does help, but I am not a huge believer in it. I'm more concerned about my state of mind, about how focus and concentration can tip a game your way at any given moment. A moment's inspiration or a human error can destroy any theory and ruin all your tactics. Coaches tend to lend greater importance to the theoretical side of the game, though, and every match they ask you for something different. Each game is different – and each coach is too. Depending on the match, they will ask you to make this movement or that one, there will be a specific order offensively or defensively, a particular position they want you to take up, an instruction to pressure the defence or to stand off …

What kind of approach the coach wants determines the way we prepare for the game during the week before. Training sessions are specifically geared towards the upcoming match, the drills we do change depending on the opponents: long diagonal balls, short one-touch passes, two on ones, crossing and finishing … there are any number of combinations.

BEFORE THE MATCH

I try not to change my pre-match ritual. I don't have a set plan that I follow but it becomes automatic. The first things I put on are my shorts and my warm-up top. Then I carefully strap up my ankles – something which is particularly important to me because I have problems with my joints there. After the physios have done their work, I put my football socks on, then I put sports socks over the top and I hold it all in place with tape. Finally, I put my shinpads on.

When it comes to coming out for matches, I do have one superstition: I always step onto the pitch right foot first, making sure I don't tread on the touchline. With Liverpool and Spain I like to come out behind the most important players. If you look you'll notice that I always come out after Jamie Carragher and Steven Gerrard. The rest of my team-mates know that and, while it's a position that a lot of them would like, they let me go out third. As for team photos, in England we only ever pose for them before Champions League games but I always stand at the back on the far left-hand side.

Concentration is very important for me. Nothing bothers me because I try to relax completely and block everything out. On the way to the stadium time can really drag so I spend my time on the coach either chatting about nothing in particular with my team-mates or listening to music on my iPod. My Spain team-mate, the Real Madrid defender Sergio Ramos, recorded a selection of songs for me during the 2006 World Cup in Germany. It's the perfect collection for the hours building up to a game and I have been listening to it ever since. I don't sing along, I just listen. Mostly they're Spanish pop songs, a bit of flamenco and the odd English ballad. Tunes that help me mentally.

Once we're in the stadium I prefer to go unnoticed. I take refuge in the dressing room. I sit on the bench, kit behind me, and chat to my team-mates or the physios and kit men. I only make an exception at European Championships or World Cups. On those occasions I like to go out and have a look at the pitch, to see what kind of state the grass is in. During this period of dead time before the game, the hands on the clock seem to move so slowly; it feels like the warm-up will never arrive. The desire to play increases and you just want to get on with it, to start concentrating on the game. Some times it's easier than others but when you look to the stands and see the fans that follow us everywhere, the adrenaline soon starts flowing.

THE WARM UP

Then there's the footballer's weapon: your boots. I have been with Nike since I was fifteen. Back in 1999, when I was playing for Atlético Madrid's youth team, we qualified to play in the Nike Premier Cup, an international tournament for clubs from around the world. That year, it was held in Italy. The biggest clubs were at the tournament: Milan, Juventus, Manchester United. We beat Real Madrid in the semi-final and then won the final against Reggina, who were the host club. I still look back on that tournament as the one that made me feel like I was nearing football's elite for the first time. And because I was voted player of the tournament, the sponsors rewarded me with a year's contract to wear their boots and clothing. I have been with them ever since.

Nike make me change boots every three months to fit in with their marketing. Because I'm superstitious, it's not something I like. I'm not happy changing when things are going well. That's why I kept wearing the same boots throughout the 2007–08 season, even though my friends at Nike, Pere Guardiola and Perfe

González, kept getting angry with me. I like to wear warm colours and I don't like black at all – more because of habit than the way they look. During Euro 2008 Nike sent us all new black boots to wear during the tournament but I ditched them in the final and wore my white ones instead – and I scored the winner. My team-mates say that I don't look right if I play or train in dark boots. After a game against PSV

Eindhoven in the Champions League, Sammy Hyypiä told me that if it hadn't been for my blond hair he wouldn't have recognised me without my white boots. The truth is, I just don't like black boots at all. Not even for training.

Making sure you're fully hydrated is very important before a game. We drink lots of isotonic energy drinks in the build-up but once I've been out for the warm up I only drink water. As we leave the pitch following the warm up we have a photo taken with the mascot and wish each other good luck. We return to the dressing room and listen to Benítez's final instructions. Then I put my shirt on and sort my hair out in front of the mirror before we leave again, ready for kick-off. At that stage, you can already hear 'You'll Never Walk Alone'. The tunnel rings with the sound of our fans. I touch the 'This is Anfield' sign and make my way down to the pitch, barely twenty metres away. Once the normal greetings are out the way, we start the final warm up with sideways runs. I like to do mine near the touchline so I can feel the excitement of the fans. When I squat down in the centre circle before the game, it's not that I'm praying or meditating, it's just something that I did once without thinking and has become a habit now. I like to look the opposition in the eye; I like to see how they're positioned, if they speak to each other and, above all, watch the fans.

AFTER THE GAME

When the referee blows the final whistle, I'm quick to return to the dressing room. I sit for five or ten minutes to recover and go back over the game in my head.

Snapshots of the match flash through your mind: a pass, a mistake, a control, a shot … There's not much time to reflect, though: almost immediately we head back out for a brief jog around the pitch before going for an ice bath. The warm-down is vital for your body to recover quickly after matches.

I tend not to take the games home with me. When I'm in the players' lounge I try to switch off completely and I try to leave everything behind when I depart the stadium. It's not fair for the people around me to have to put up with me being in a good or bad mood depending on the result – and besides, at Liverpool we almost always win. But it's not easy. If we have lost, I don't want to do anything. Luckily, there's a game every three days so if you've played badly, you almost immediately have the chance to make up for it. Win or lose, one thing I never miss are the highlights on television. After the derby with Everton at Anfield in 2008–09, I kept on replaying it over and over. It finished 1–1 and I had hit the post after a long ball from Sami Hyypia. It reached the point where Olalla had to say to me: 'You've seen it enough; stop going round and round in circles.' She was right but it was important for us to win and we had lost the three points late in the game from a set play. Cahill's goal really hurt me because I felt responsible for us not winning. I felt that I had not done enough to help out my team-mates, so I went over and over it until we won the next match.

I'm not one for special goal celebrations. I prefer to be spontaneous, although I do sometimes having something planned – like when I dedicate goals to my nephews Hugo and Paula or to my friends' kids. Normally, though, I just like to run towards the fans and see the happiness in their faces. That's the best reward I could ask for. Then I seek out Olalla in the crowd and blow her a kiss. I'm not one for wearing messages scribbled on a t-shirt under my shirt either, not least because I tend to wear a thermal sports top underneath. I did make an exception once though. It was in the spring of 2001 and I was playing for Spain in the Junior European Championships in England. Underneath my Spain shirt I had a t-shirt with the words 'Andrés, that's for you' written on it. We were playing France in the final and Andrés Iniesta, who's now at Barcelona, had suffered an injury and couldn't play. I scored a penalty and ran over to the bench where he was to show him the message. It was the winning goal – and it was for him.

X

'Spanish' Liverpool

One of the first things I was told
when I arrived in England was
not to take the easy way out and
respond with a simple 'yes' or 'no'
if I didn't understand what
people were saying to me.

was told to be honest and say: 'I didn't catch that, could you say it again?' but the truth is I didn't always take that advice. I nearly always just mumbled a 'no'. That's what I did whenever I was in the supermarket and was asked if I wanted 'cashback'. It's not something we have in Spain and I had no idea what it was. It was three months before I knew what they were talking about.

Luckily, getting used to the city and its people was easier than learning the language. With so many Spanish speakers in the dressing room – not just the Spanish and Argentinian players but also Yossi Benayoun, Fabio Aurelio and Momo Sissoko, all of whom had played in Spain, plus the coaching staff – there were days when even trying to have a conversation in English wasn't easy. At first, I took refuge in that Spanish-speaking group because it was really hard to understand what people were saying to me in English. Pepe Reina, who is my neighbour as well as a team-mate for club and country, was the man who helped me the most. And of course having Rafa Benítez there really helped me not to feel lost on the pitch. I was grateful that he could give me vital instructions in Spanish.

Curiously enough, the tables have turned now. When I play for Spain, I find myself communicating with Xabi Alonso and other team-mates in English. It's instinctive, an automatic reaction. Sometimes I'll shout instructions as if we were back in England. Out on the pitch, some words seem to carry better in English than Spanish.

Two people were vital during my first few days in the city: Rob and Alan, the English teachers Liverpool laid on for me. We tried to fit classes around matches and training sessions. At first we were doing at least two hours at a time, three days a week, but as I improved the classes became less frequent. Soon, I was only doing two a week. I enjoyed it a lot and time passed quickly. One of the things they used to make me do was ring people up in response to adverts in the paper. You'd get on the phone and ask about a puppy for sale, or that kitten being advertised, or the price of a second-hand car. The idea was to get me used to speaking in English on the phone but at first the idea terrified me. So much so that I would panic when I didn't understand something and find myself having to run to Pepe Reina.

The car radio became my constant travelling companion. Every morning on my way to training at Melwood, I would listen and try to concentrate on what was being said. At first I only understood a few words but bit by bit I could feel myself improving. As I went past billboards I would try to translate them, too, and with every passing day I was getting better and better. Some nights, I even dared to pick up the phone and order food. When it turned up, it was nearly always what I wanted.

When we were in hotels preparing for games I watched films in English with the subtitles on. I remember that the first film I watched was *The Illusionist*. The first time round, I didn't understand a thing but when I watched it again a few months later, I found that I could follow virtually the whole film perfectly. Sometimes I'd lose track of the dialogue and have to rewind and listen to it again, but it worked. The other thing I always carried with me was 'English Training' on my Nintendo DS – language games and exercises that helped me develop my English.

You don't just need to be able to speak English off the pitch. On the pitch it's absolutely vital to be able to communicate properly. Your relationship with referees improves if you can speak to them and that language barrier is one you have to overcome. You also need to be able to communicate quickly and effectively with your team-mates during the game and in training. Pretty much the first four phrases I learnt in English were 'Time', 'Man On', 'Turn' and 'Over'. That's what I mean when I say I speak to Xabi Alonso in English even when we are playing for Spain: they're such quick, clear commands and they become so ingrained that you find yourself saying them instinctively without thinking.

Xabi probably spoke the best English of all the Spaniards at Liverpool before he left. He even confidently answered questions in English on the day of his presentation. The Everton player Mikel Arteta, who's a good friend, speaks very good English too, just like Pepe and Albert Riera; Álvaro Arbeloa, now at Real Madrid, was good too; and I'm progressing well.

The list of those who speak Spanish is a long one. There's Mascherano, Insúa, Fabio Aurelio, Lucas Leiva, Benayoun, a whole load of reserve-team players, like Francis, Pacheco, Ayala, San José, Bruna, and all of Benítez's coaching staff: Sammy Lee, who played for Osasuna in Spain, Pellegrino, Paco de Miguel, Xavi Valero ... Even so, whenever you're with anyone who doesn't speak Spanish, you speak English. It's English that dominates. I think that's logical. We live in England and play for an English club.

One of the many times Pepe had to save me from making a fool of myself came just after we had arrived in Hong Kong, where we had gone on tour following pre-season training in Switzerland. Alex Miller, who was Benítez's assistant at the time, told us that we had to change into our training gear ready for a light session to get used to the conditions there. Seeing that I didn't seem to be taking much notice, Pepe turned to me and said: 'Do you know what he said?' I replied that, yes,

he'd said that as our training gear hadn't yet arrived we wouldn't be training. You could hear Pepe laughing all the way round the hotel. 'No,' Pepe replied, 'he said, get up to your room, get changed, and get to training.' I got in the lift, up to my room and the training kit was there. I got changed and it was off to work.

My room-mate in Hong Kong was Momo Sissoko, which enabled me to overcome the language barrier because he spoke Spanish, having been at Valencia. In Switzerland, where my room-mate was Steve Finnan, it was a different story. His patience was unbelievable. We used to go from the hotel to the training pitch by bike each morning. One day after the session, I stayed on for a while doing some stretches when I suddenly realised that my team-mates had gone back to the hotel without me. Determined to catch up, I grabbed my bike and started pedalling away furiously. In the wrong direction. Before I knew it, I was lost. I had no idea which direction the hotel was in or where I was going and ended up going round and round

the town until I passed a corner that looked familiar. Eventually I walked into the foyer, still with the bike. I couldn't find the place I was supposed to leave it either.

One place you can't afford to get it wrong is at the doctors'. You have to be very careful. If you don't explain your symptoms properly, you can end up being given the wrong treatment. If you can't explain exactly where the pain is, and what kind of pain it is, it can hinder your rehabilitation. I think my English improved quicker in the physios' room than anywhere else because I really concentrated on memorising phrases and learning when to use them. I also had one big advantage, mind you: a Spanish physio called Víctor Salinas.

As I said, at first I was terrified at the prospect of having to have a conversation on the phone. Imagine how much worse it is when that conversation is with the fire service. My smoke alarm kept going off in the house I was renting and one afternoon I got a call. I just about worked out that the man on the other end was from the local fire station but I didn't understand anything else. A few minutes later, a fire engine turned up at the house, packed with fireman thinking they were being called into action. They came three times in three days before they worked out that the smoke from cooking was causing the alarm to go off prematurely. The next time the alarm went off, they called me first to check whether they really did have to set off again.

XI
A bitter taste

It had all begun so well that it could have been written by the most optimistic of scriptwriters on a Hollywood action movie: a debut at the Calderón, a goal and a victory at Albacete, almost the whole of the second half against Sporting at home … and now it was all set up for the perfect happy ending with the chance to win promotion to La Liga on the final day of the 2000–01 season.

T here were three teams fighting it out for two promotion places. The problem was that Betis and Tenerife – led by Rafa Benítez and boasting Luis García, both of whom would later end up at Liverpool – had their destiny in their own hands. We didn't. We won but so did they and we were condemned to another season in the Second Division – on goal difference. During the previous summer, Atlético had launched an advertising campaign to increase morale and make sure the fans were on our side despite being relegated. The slogan ran: 'One little year in hell: Manchester United and Milan have been here too.' Sadly, one little year turned into two.

I had been a professional footballer for barely twenty days. I had played four matches and already I had my first, bitter taste of disappointment. And yet the feeling that washed over me was that of a fan who had just become a footballer. It was too soon to truly consider myself one of them, part of the team. I was aware of how difficult it was to return to the top flight but the huge disappointment of not going up only really hit me hard for a few minutes when I contemplated the possibility that the slip-up could halt my progress, stopping me in my tracks when I had only just begun. I experienced the failure to win promotion privately and in silence. I was a novice who had swapped his scarf for the No. 35 shirt, his jeans for Atlético shorts and a pair of trainers for football boots. I was an Atlético fan who had been given the chance to help out his team … but I hadn't been able to help enough for us to win promotion.

Most of my team-mates returned to the dressing room in tears. Their faces were a picture of despair. But we had not been a failure. It's only a failure when you haven't done everything you can to win and those players had given their all on the pitch at Getafe, where the dream of promotion slipped away.

Witnessing a devastated dressing room packed with players who had won so much filled me with sadness. I could barely raise my eyes from the tiles on the floor. Kiko Narváez, Toni Muñoz, Juanma López and Carlos Aguilera looked at each other in search of support. Juan Gómez, his leg in plaster, bit his lip to stop himself crying. It was a desperate scene. The silence was frightening. We had been torn apart. The fans might not have seen it like this, but we cared. We wanted to find ourselves at a party not a funeral – more than anyone else. And for some of the senior players the taste of defeat was even more bitter. Having failed to win promotion, their next step was to leave the club through the back door.

The day of the game had been madness. Huge numbers of Atlético fans travelled down to Getafe in convoy. Getafe, about 15km south of Madrid, was a sea of red and white. It was as if it was a home game for us. Meanwhile, those Atlético fans who couldn't get tickets for our game also made the short journey south: this time to the neighbouring town of Leganés, where Tenerife were playing Leganés. Just south of Madrid, in two satellite towns bordering the country's capital, barely 5km apart, promotion was played out. All week, fans had just been waiting for Sunday to come, the tension growing with every minute. On the day, there was hope and excitement in the air. And the word coming through on the radio had everyone believing it was possible. We were winning in Getafe; a few kilometres away in Leganés, Tenerife were only drawing.

Carlos García Cantarero had included me in the starting XI for the first time. In the three previous games I had come off the bench. This time I was up front with Salva Ballesta, a former striker at Sevilla, Valencia and Bolton. But just when things were going so well, a strange, almost impossible goal in Leganés, aided by an unusual mistake from the goalkeeper, put Tenerife in the lead and back in the promotion positions. In Getafe, news came through and the stands fell silent. Where there had been shouts and chants, it went quiet. And you really felt it out on the pitch. We knew. No one had to tell me that we were going to be spending another year in hell. Fifteen days earlier I had witnessed the wonderful side of football with a goal and victory in Albacete and the fans celebrating as if we had won promotion. Now, I was experiencing the other side of the coin: tears and sadness as we clinched a victory that was worthless; the party had become a funeral. In the dressing room the only sound was made by the kit men as they went round picking things up and packing away; in the bus on the way back to the Vicente Calderón, the silence was even more acute. No one uttered a single word.

I left the Calderón to cheers and applause. Around a hundred fans had come down to our stadium to have a go at the players. Well, some of them. I was one of the exceptions. By praising me, they found another way of attacking some of the veteran players and of telling the owners that they should have trusted in youth more. As I got into the car with my dad to the sound of applause I could see that it was a very different story for some of my team-mates: they faced insults and even missiles being thrown at their car windows. Some of the more radical fans used sticks and hit players' cars as they went by. The sense of helplessness at another season in the Second Division had seen some of them lose control completely.

The journey home to Fuenlabrada seemed to take forever. Only the radio broke the silence. My dad had chosen a station where, inevitably, they were talking about football. When we got home I went straight to my room. Once I had closed the door and found myself alone, the sadness engulfed me. I had tried to stay strong but looking round at the photos and pictures on my wall, I couldn't prevent a tear escaping.

Our season wasn't yet over, though – and that made it harder still. We had a two-legged Copa del Rey semi-final ahead of us against Real Zaragoza. I didn't really know what to do with myself, what to say, where to go. But I carried on just like any other player. I could see the desire for revenge in the players' eyes: they did not want to pass up the opportunity to reach the final. We were 180 minutes away and everyone was really determined as we came out onto the pitch at the Calderón for the first leg. We started like a whirlwind, really flying into our opponents and creating a number of clear chances. I started the match and felt good: we had begun well and were convinced we could win. But when things were going well, some of the most radical ultras in the South Stand started throwing rubber balls at the players on the pitch. It went on for about 20 minutes and the referee was forced to stop the game. Our momentum was gone. Immediately after the restart, we gave away a free-kick that led to a red card. Zaragoza scored from the free-kick. In barely ten minutes, everything had gone down the pan. Cantarero took me off as he sought to strengthen our defence following the red card. We ended up losing 2–0.

I was back in the starting XI for the second leg in Zaragoza. Four minutes into the game, I was fouled in the penalty area but the referee refused to point to the spot. As I fell, I damaged my collar bone. After everything that had happened, I finished my first season in a hospital in Zaragoza accompanied by Dr Villalón, the club doctor, with my arm in a sling. I watched the last few minutes of our match from the bench at the Romareda alongside our captain Toni, who had also picked up an injury in his last ever game as a professional. We won 1–0 but it wasn't enough to reach the final of the Copa del Rey.

It was time for me to reflect on two frenetic months. I needed a break. I needed to get used to the fact that things would never be the same again. All the more so after the sporting director Paulo Futre told me that I would be permanently joining the first-team squad the following season. In less than twenty days, I would be back with Atlético and working under Luis Aragonés, who had just been named the new coach. A club legend as player and coach, he had been entrusted with the job of taking us back to the top flight. At the same time, the club announced which players would be leaving. Toni, López and Kiko, three of the players who won the club's historic league and cup double, had played their last game for Atlético. Toni and López had played their last game for any club, in fact, and were set to hang up their boots. Kiko, my childhood idol, was leaving home after eight years. Of the veterans in the squad only Carlos Aguilera, whom I would later share the captaincy with, survived the cull.

My holidays were as strange as the sight of me wearing a makeshift sling on my right arm. Just before heading off to Galicia I stopped by the offices at the Calderón to pick up the holiday training programme that had been put together for me which included exercises to strengthen the area around my collar bone. Dr Villalón also wanted to have a look at the injury in the clinic under the stands. One of the employees there mentioned that Luis Aragonés's assistant was in the stadium, preparing pre-season training. I didn't know Jesús Paredes personally but I vaguely remembered his face from photographs. I decided to look for him and introduce myself. I came across a group of staff members having a chat in one of the corridors. As I got closer to them, one said: 'Hi Fernando, how's the injury?' 'Getting better, thanks,' I replied. 'I'm looking for Jesús Paredes.' There was a voice from the group: 'You've found him.'

XII
Adiós, Atlético

A lot has been said about the night in May 2007 that Barcelona beat Atlético Madrid 6–0 at the Vicente Calderón and whether that result made up my mind to leave.

The answer is yes: that night was a turning point. I tried to push it from my mind. The following day I even went through with a trip that I had planned to visit a school in Toledo, 60km south of Madrid. I didn't want to break a promise. The last time I had visited, I told them that when I reached 25 caps with Spain I would go and visit the pupils again. But, although I was surrounded by kids and keeping myself occupied, it was no good: the game with Barcelona never ended. I went over it again and again in my head.

When I finally came to a conclusion, it struck me. I reflected on the match and could not avoid the sense that Barcelona were a big club and Atlético were not yet. They were still making the transition towards becoming a big club again. I would have liked the roles to have been reversed; I would have liked Atlético to have been the team that steamrollered their way through the match; I would have liked Barcelona's players to be the ones trudging back to the dressing room, heads down. But that was just a dream; the reality was very different. I asked myself how long it would be before that became possible. The thought went round my head and I reached the conclusion that to compete with Barcelona – to really compete, as equals – we'd need five to eight years. Two or three years would never be enough to reach their level. I also thought Atlético needed to build a team without focusing entirely on just one player.

The atmosphere in the stadium that night against Barcelona was strange. If Atlético beat Barcelona they would be helping Real Madrid in the fight for the 2006–07 league title. The fans were divided. Some wanted to win and not even think about other teams. Others wanted to lose because they knew that it would damage their most hated rivals. When I left the Calderón after being hammered it occurred to me that those clubs whose fans prefer to see another team struggle than their own team win are destined to forever live in the shadow of other teams' success. The men responsible for what happened were the players. We hadn't been able to make it clear to our supporters that they should want their team to win and ignore the issue of whether or not the result favoured Real. During my time at Atlético we as players never managed to do justice to the club's history. That 6–0 defeat brought home just how far we were from what I wanted the club to be.

Four weeks after the defeat against Barcelona, we qualified for the Intertoto Cup. In the time between 20 May, when we played Barcelona, and 17 June, when the season ended, I had taken a call from Rafa Benítez at Liverpool but had not heard any more and thought nothing of it. After beating Osasuna on the final day, the Atlético Madrid owner Miguel-Ángel Gil asked me about my future while we were waiting for a flight at Pamplona airport. He wanted to know where I saw myself next season. He was aware of the offer from England. It wasn't the time or the place to be having the conversation so we agreed to meet at the Calderón the following morning. And that was how I found myself in the owner's office asking him to listen to Liverpool's offer.

I have always had a respectful and cordial relationship with Atlético's majority shareholder. As captain of the club, I have had conversations with him on every subject and we got on well. He had asked me to continue at Atlético so many times; now, it was my turn to ask him to try to come to an agreement with Liverpool that would benefit all of us. I explained to him that, after giving it a lot of thought, I felt that my time at Atlético had come to an end and it was the right moment to move on. I needed a new challenge. Gil told me that he understood my position but that he wouldn't give me away. He agreed to negotiate with Benítez but said that he wouldn't make it easy for the Liverpool manager because, he explained, I was the most valuable asset the club had and it was his duty to get a big fee for me. I reminded him that I had come through the club's youth system and asked him to be fair.

Given what Gil had said, I thought that we would be in for a long, tedious summer of negotiation but just 48 hours later I was told that the two clubs had come to an agreement. I was surprised at how quickly they had been able to shake hands on a deal and I decided to send Gil a message on his mobile to thank him for having listened. I still wasn't a Liverpool player, though, because I hadn't spoken to them about the terms of my contract. That's when Margarita Garay, one of my representatives at Bahía Internacional and someone I trust entirely, set to work. A few days later a seven-year deal was agreed that would make me a Liverpool player until 30 June 2013. I had been granted my wish.

Despite everything that had happened, I wasn't fully aware of just how big a step I had taken. I was on holiday in Haiti and I didn't know if I was happy or sad, or both.

I took a call that I had been told to expect. Benítez was on the other end. It was the second time I had spoken to him on the phone. He told me that everything had been agreed, pending the medical. Until the doctors gave the okay, we had to wait. Although my agents had told him that I was away on holiday, Benítez asked me to get back as soon as possible to undertake the medical. I was thousands of miles away and, even if I managed to get the quickest flight connections possible, at least 24 hours from Madrid. Yet Benítez wanted me to be in Liverpool the following morning. It wasn't possible; it took me a few days to get the tickets together to fly home. I grew increasingly excited and impatient. The expectation was growing. But I still didn't know what lay ahead.

My ankle was in a bad, bad way. I had played the last two games of the season against Celta and Osasuna with an injury following a sprain I'd picked up in training with the Spain squad in Las Rozas. Because I was on holiday I hadn't had the chance to do any proper rehabilitation. So when I saw Mark Waller, the Liverpool doctor, and the look on his face, I was nervous. The first part of the medical took place in one of the rooms of the apartment that the club had put me in alongside the Mersey. I didn't speak English and the doctor didn't speak any Spanish but I could tell that things weren't going well. His expression after looking at my ankle gave the game away. He then made me support my body weight on the damaged ankle. I couldn't stand up. Within half an hour, I was on my way to hospital for a proper scan.

I had only seen Liverpool through the window of a car. The plane landed at Liverpool airport's private terminal, so I didn't cross paths with any fans. Because

everything still depended on the medical, both clubs wanted to maintain confidentiality. Not that it made much difference: the media were already talking about me leaving Atlético Madrid for Liverpool. I didn't speak to any journalists in England. Liverpool even asked me to eat privately in the apartment rather than going out for a meal. From there I headed to the medical centre, where they were waiting for me. Benítez called me again. 'What's happening with your ankle?' he asked. 'What the doctor said worried me.' I explained what had happened and he told me that Dr Waller wanted to do some tests to see if the ligament was damaged. After two hours of tests, Dr Waller gave me an approving look. Jorge Lera translated as, test results in hand, Dr Waller explained what the situation was. 'You're going to have to go through a long period of rehab with the physio,' Jorge said. His smile was designed to ease the tension of the previous few hours.

A few hours earlier, during the first part of the medical that morning, Liverpool told me that they planned to present me to the media before I'd had a chance to say goodbye to Atlético. The idea, approved by Benítez, was to do the presentation on Tuesday 3 July. But I wanted to make sure I did things the right way. I rang Rafa to explain how I wanted to handle things.

'They said you want to do my presentation before I've said goodbye at Atlético,' I said.

'Yes,' he replied, 'that makes sense: as of today, you'll be a Liverpool player.'

'Sure, but first I want to say goodbye to the Atlético fans,' I continued. 'This is a big and difficult step for me. I have to say goodbye first. I've been there my whole life, they've always treated me wonderfully and they deserve a proper farewell. I have to show them my gratitude before I go. I can't pull on another team's shirt without having explained my reasons for going first.'

Rafa understood. That same night we flew back to Madrid, while an announcement was made: the following morning at 10am, I would give a press conference at the Vicente Calderón to say goodbye to Atlético; the following afternoon at 3pm I would give another press conference at Anfield to say hello to Liverpool.

It was then that I started to feel a little more like a Liverpool player. The transfer was made public, I got welcome messages from Gerrard and Carragher, and the phone started ringing with people wishing me luck. I ate with my family and slept

well. I didn't know what awaited me the following day; I had no idea what my future would bring. The night went by quickly and by 9.30am the following morning I was at the Calderón. It was then that it dawned on me, that I realised what the step I had taken meant. In the car park, I could see the faces of my friends and family. I walked towards the offices, passing people I have known since I was a kid. Alberto, Charo, Briñas, Santi… the look in their eyes was a sad one but there was gratitude in their silence. The way they were clearly feeling really touched me. It hurt. Every look was a memory; every second was a hammer blow that left me thinking: you're leaving all this behind. The fans were waiting by the gates to the stadium, unable to get in. There was no way back.

During the press conference, I looked at my family, at the friends who had come to support me, and at the club employees who had shared the journey with me for so many years. People who would wait for me to say goodbye properly. I held it

together as best I could but I was really struggling. I just wanted that press conference to be over as soon as possible. People questioned my reasons, they doubted what I said, but the message I gave was the truth. I respected the people who understood my reasons for going and I respected those who did not even more. I had been a fan too; I remember taking the departure of Christian Vieri, our top scorer in the late 1990s, really badly. When he went back to Italy, I thought it was the end of the world. That's why I understood those people who didn't like my decision to leave as much as those who supported me in it. When the press conference finished, I could see the sadness in lots of people's eyes; others were looking at me, trying to hold back the tears. It was harder than I could have ever imagined.

I have always admired players who have been at the same club for their entire career. Players like Gerrard, Raúl and Totti are an example. That was my dream too. Over more than 12 years at Atlético, my dream had been to finish my career there. On the few occasions I even contemplated leaving, the idea seemed improbable and distant. I never went back on my idea. I always wanted to stay at Atlético Madrid because there's no place like home. But when I analysed my career coldly, there was no escaping the fact that my best years would coincide with a transitional period at Atlético as they sought to get back to where they once belonged. I had had offers to leave before but never listened. Benítez's call made me rethink. I had decided that now it was time to leave.

Time has proven that it was the right decision for everyone: Atlético have grown and I have too. Other players will be the stars and reach heights that I could not. As for the fans, I am happy because they understood my decision. People tell me that when you go to the Calderón you see lots of Liverpool shirts with my name and number. It was the right decision and a successful one. A kind of brotherhood has even emerged between Atlético fans and Liverpool supporters. The Champions League match between the two sides in 2008, which I had to miss because of injury, helped to forge a union – for them and for me. I was born, grew up and developed as a footballer in Madrid; I took off in Liverpool. Liverpool and Atlético will always walk together in my heart.

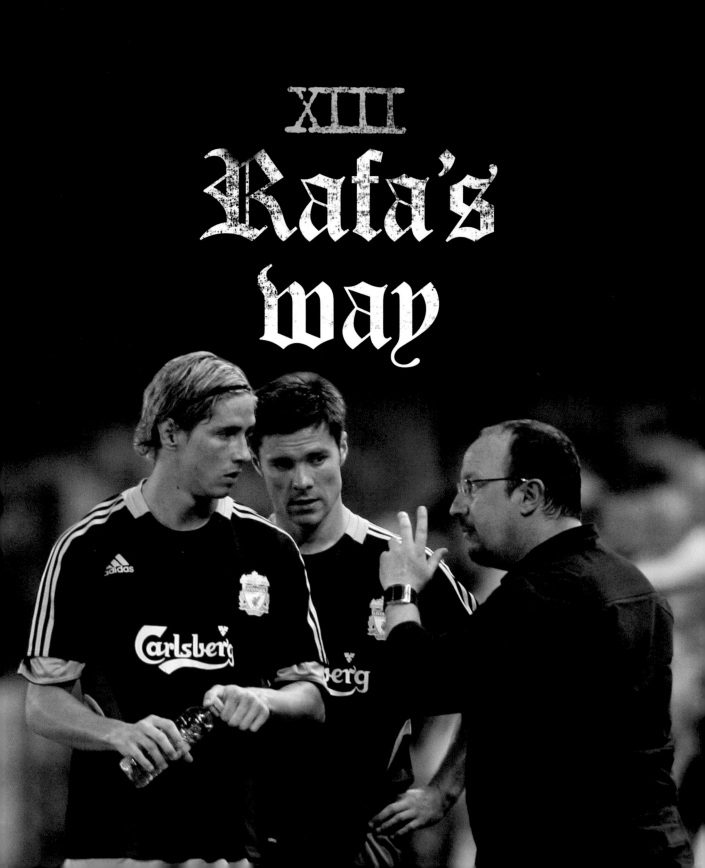

XIII
Rafa's way

Winter on Merseyside, a cold February morning at Melwood. There are smiling faces everywhere, jokes fly around the dressing room. It's a Monday morning and everyone is happy. We've just beaten Chelsea and we're still in the fight for the Premier League title.

I'm doing up my boots ready to head out to the training pitch when the manager Rafa Benítez comes over. During the previous few days the papers have been full of stories about me becoming a father. 'Congratulations Fernando,' Rafa says. 'Thanks boss,' I reply.

I assumed that he was congratulating me on the pregnancy and I paused, expecting the obvious next question: How's the mother? Or: Will it be a girl or a boy? I was wrong. I'd forgotten that the man standing in front of me was a coach who thinks about football 24 hours a day, seven days a week. 'Just as we'd anticipated, attacking the near post really paid off yesterday,' he said. 'You got ahead of the defender into that space we talked about, which gave you an advantage and allowed to you beat Cech with a header. It was a good pass from Fabio but you worked it well. Congratulations.' And with that, Rafa turned and headed out for training.

Rafa Benítez, football coach. A football coach through and through. A man absolutely dedicated to a difficult, demanding and often ungrateful profession. The first time I knew anything of his work was when he was at Tenerife and I was taking my first steps at Atlético Madrid. They were our rivals for promotion from the Second Division. I had only been in the first team for three games and we were battling it out head to head with them for promotion. Sevilla were already up and Betis were practically there. We were playing in Getafe and Tenerife were playing in Leganés on the final day and it was Tenerife who went up.

I wasn't surprised when Valencia signed him that summer. Years later, I was told a story about that season. Benítez's Valencia were playing Espanyol in Barcelona on a Saturday night. The Valencia president rang the B-team coach César Ferrando and asked him to be reachable the following day because, he said, 'if we lose we're going to sack Benítez'. They didn't lose. They won. César stayed where he was and Benítez ended up winning the league, which is when I really started to take notice. I realised then that he always sent his teams out with a very clear style and just one mission: to compete. With a smaller budget they beat the biggest teams. There might not have been much raw material but Benítez had formed an almost unbeatable unit. Benítez builds teams that win matches – and titles.

When I was with the Spanish national team, I wondered about Benítez, about how he worked, what his training sessions were like, what his methods were, what he was like with the players, what his system was, what rules he imposed ... José Manuel Ochotorena, who had gone to Liverpool from Valencia with Benítez, was Spain's goalkeeping coach too. I was forever asking him and my friend Pepe Reina what Benítez was like. The idea that I might work for him one day never crossed my mind but I used to joke with Pepe saying: 'Tell him to sign me.' So much so, in fact, that by the fourth question Pepe would respond with a threat: 'Carry on like that and I will tell him, you'll see! You're a pain!' For those who think that sounds like I was already angling for a move, I wasn't. It hadn't even occurred to me that it might be a genuine possibility. I used to bore Cesc Fàbregas with questions about Wenger too. English football fascinated me.

After the Champions League final in Athens, in late May 2007, the Spanish national team met again at the Federation's training ground in Las Rozas, just outside Madrid. We had Euro 2008 qualifying games against Liechtenstein and Latvia coming up. During the morning session, Sergio Ramos fell on top of me and I twisted my right ankle. I suffered a grade 2 sprain and was sent back to Atlético to work on my rehabilitation with the physios there in an attempt to be fit for two key games we had left, against Celta and Osasuna, in the battle to qualify for the Uefa Cup. While I was working on my fitness, my phone rang twice in two days. Both times, it was the same number – an English number. And both times, I ignored it. I don't pick up the phone if I don't recognise the number. When I got a third call from the same English number while we were out walking the dogs, I joked to Olalla: 'That'll be Benítez wanting to sign me.' In the end, curiosity got the better of me – after all, whoever it was had been very insistent – and that evening, a Sunday night, I rang back. There was no answer but a couple of seconds later whoever it was returned the call.

'Hello Fernando,' said a Spanish voice at the other end, 'do you know who this is?'

'No,' I replied.

'You mean, you'd ring a random English number when you don't even know who it is?' the voice said.

'Not normally, no,' I said, 'but I've had three calls from this number and I want to know who it is.'

'It's Rafa Benítez ...'

There wasn't much conversation – not from me, at least. My responses were to the point, short and cold. Too cold. Off-hand. I'm amazed he didn't tell me to get lost. My mind was racing, trying to place the voice, to decide if it really was Benítez. But how should I know when I had never spoken to him before? He didn't stop talking. He explained what his plans were and he told me that he had decided that I was the player he wanted to be Liverpool's centre-forward. He needed to

know if I was committed enough to the idea for him to fight for my signature and start negotiating with Atlético Madrid. I didn't know what to say. I hadn't had time to think; my mind wasn't clear, it was spinning. I was thinking that maybe it was a mate of mine fooling around or some impersonator trying to catch me out. I thought I might be falling victim to another bad taste joke, like José Antonio Reyes when someone from a radio station rang him pretending to be Real Madrid's vice-president Emilio Butragueño while he was still at Arsenal and he got himself in all sorts of trouble by admitting to 'Butragueño' that he would love to join Madrid.

Almost all I managed to say was 'Speak to Miguel Ángel Gil, Atlético's owner, and when the league's over I'll think about my future.'

Benítez is a manager who knows how to get the best out of his players. He knows how to choose the right players for his system, players who fit his philosophy for the team and the squad. He builds a strong group and helps to improve the individual within it. He pushes you so hard that you end up playing at 120% of your potential. Then he pushes you some more. Once he has got you playing at your very peak, he finds a way to fit all the pieces together for maximum effect. He is really insistent on every little detail. From the inside you really notice the work he does; from the outside you notice a team that works hard, a team that is a real collective unit, that plays with pace, always ready to launch a counter-attack from any part of the pitch, including its own penalty area. There is complete solidarity between all the players and absolute trust in the coach. He has built a team in his own image: serious, dedicated, organised, committed. His touch has helped make us mentally strong but without ever losing humility or our work ethic.

Rafa lives football 24 hours a day. He's meticulous and so insistent on the small details that it can be hard to deal with. He's so on top of you that a lot of the time he's on the pitch reminding you of your mistakes the second the game is over, while he normally ignores the things you did well.

He encourages you with criticism, pushing you to improve every day. If you can't handle that, it can damage your self-esteem, but if you can handle it, it pushes you on. He knows that only hard work, the constant desire to improve, can make you a better player. He provides you with information and details you didn't even know about and hadn't even noticed but that help you get better. He lays great store by the geometry of football: where you are in relation to the ball, if you're half a metre further forward or half a metre further back ... The work you do and the improvements that come with it gives you confidence. So does he. During my first few weeks at Liverpool I could have let the doubts really get to me because I hadn't managed to score in pre-season but he kept me calm and made me see that what was happening was normal, that progress was being made.

The tactical work done by Liverpool's coaching staff makes an important appearance during the pre-match team talks. We have video sessions where they explain strategic points and highlight the opposition's weaknesses. Rafa likes to encourage dialogue. He doesn't want to just show us a video, talk on his own and then jump on the bus to go to the ground. He asks the players for their opinion and tries to involve them in the debate over what we should do. Sometimes he even interrogates you about your role or some move you're supposed to carry out. Sometimes, I feel like I'm back being a schoolboy in Fuenlabrada with a teacher testing me on what he's just taught us. I remember that during one of the first team talks I was involved in he asked us, in a word, what the key to winning the game was. It was my turn to answer. I couldn't think of anything; I was racking my brain but drawing blanks when Yossi Benayoun rescued me with a whisper in my ear: 'Pass'. My English wasn't great at that stage and sometimes I couldn't find the words that I was looking for. That was another area where Benítez was important, in fact. It's not true that he fines you or punishes you for speaking in Spanish but he does insist on the importance of learning English, to help you understand and integrate. He's right too. If there are three Spanish speakers talking, even if one of them is Rafa, then of course we'll speak in Spanish. But if anyone else joins the conversation we immediately switch to English.

During team talks you realise just how closely Benítez studies the opposition. He likes to tell us the line up when we get to the dressing room but even before that he has given a tactical lesson in how the other team plays. Even though he doesn't want us to know what team we're going to play, he insists on us knowing what team the opposition will play. He will select his team and his tactics depending on the opposition and the specific needs of the game in question. Against Real Madrid in the Champions League, he approached the two games in completely different ways, even though he had the same players available. He knows that he has footballers who are versatile and can adapt to various ways of playing. That allows him to do the same. He's very clear about what he wants – a win – and the best way to go about getting it at any given moment. Because of that, he has his critics – but what is 'good football'? Playing two hundred passes? Sometimes it's better to play just three passes and get into the opposition's penalty area quickly. Benítez is not a defensive coach or a boring one. He is faithful to his ideas and he will not change, no matter how much pressure people put on him. He is proactive, he doesn't sit and wait. Instead, he makes us play in the best possible way to make sure we win.

Benítez does a lot of individual work with the players too. Not only does he make sure you never take your foot off the pedal, he also works to iron out the small defects in your game. He was the one that specifically wanted me to join Liverpool and right from the start he has made me undergo personal drills to help me tactically and technically. With Ryan Babel and Dirk Kuyt, for example, we work on drills to improve our control, passing and movement to make sure the team always has useful options with which to build moves and launch attacks. He gives us short, enjoyable exercises to complete: ways of positioning ourselves in front of goal, how to improve our movement tactically, and how to gauge our energy and reserve it accordingly. I think I run less now than I did. But because I run more intelligently, I get more of the ball. That's a result of experience – and hours of hard work.

I honestly don't think I have ever had a conversation with Benítez that hasn't been about football. That's just the way he is.

XIV

Through the lens

I never thought I'd become an icon.
When I was younger, the idea of me being
the face of a multi-national company
or appearing in adverts would have
sounded like a joke. But it has happened.
Not that I would ever compare myself to
Michael Jordan or David Beckham.
They are unique, inimitable. The rest
of us can only follow in their footsteps.
We could never match them. They were
the ones that opened the way for
sportsmen to become the focus for
international advertising campaigns.

Torres
el Niño

$\mathfrak{I}$ don't especially enjoy the filming and photoshoots that adverts entail. At first the novelty made it fun but in the end it becomes an obligation, a bit of a chore. That said, I have never missed a single training session because of a photoshoot; I have always been adamant that commercial commitments will not affect my game in any way. It's a case of taking advantage of my free time to do something different. To be honest, I feel a little embarrassed when I see myself on billboards, in adverts on television or promoting a product. But I am aware that it represents a good source of income and helps to increase your public profile.

For a long time now, people have speculated over the meaning behind my changing look or latest haircut. There was no meaning: it was just a matter of taste and age. No one advised me to go for this haircut or that, it was all instinctive. I'd wake up one morning and feel like a change, like trying something new – just like any 18- or 20-year-old would do. The difference was that people saw me on television. And it is not as if I would stand there in front of the mirror every day, either. It depended on how I felt. Doing adverts puts you in the public eye and draws criticism, especially if you are a footballer. People seem to think players' performances on the pitch dip according to how many commercials they are doing; as if there is a direct correlation between the number of photoshoots you've done and the way you play. Some people seem more interested in analysing our lives off the pitch and the adverts we do than whether we act well or badly on the pitch.

In England, not so much is made of it. Since I have been at Liverpool, I have found that people take my commercial commitments in their stride. It's considered normal. It's seen as something sportsmen do and the criticism is not so fierce as it can be in Spain. I don't know if Beckham changed people's perspective or if it was already like that before he came on the scene. What I do know is that I am convinced that getting involved with publicity campaigns does not affect your performance as a footballer. If I wasn't convinced of that, I wouldn't get involved.

The first big advert I did, the one that really opened doors for me, was in the spring of 2004 for Pepe Jeans, a modern and innovative clothing company that was

founded in the early 1970s in Portobello market in east London. I had to pose with my shirt off, alongside the model Leticia Birkheuer for an ambitious international campaign that, they later told me, proved to be a big success. The sessions were carried out in a stone quarry in the province of Guadalajara, about 100km north of Madrid, and I have to say I was surprised at how patient I managed to be. After all, it was all new to me. It wasn't like the photoshoots I had done before with my football sponsors Nike, or the sessions that I had been involved in for magazines and newspapers, when I would have to pose for half an hour at Atlético's training ground. This was completely different.

I had to pose for a world-famous fashion photographer, surrounded by a fifty-strong team of assistants. It was much more serious than anything I had been used to and so new that I barely had time to think about it or even get nervous: I was swept along by the novelty and excitement of it. The only problem was communicating with the photographer, who was an American. A translator had to explain some of the poses to me and I think it soon became clear that I was a footballer, not a model. One of the things that most surprised me was when they tried to cut my hair. 'The director said I have to,' the stylist told me. 'Well, tell him I said no,' I replied, a bit taken aback. It struck me as strange but I later leant that it's no more unusual than them testing the light. I couldn't help but smile when they showed me the photos Cristiano Ronaldo had done for the same brand – and wonder whether he had gone through the same trials and tribulations that I had.

I have always been adamant that I will never pose for a photo that might damage my profession. Football fans could get the wrong impression about me and I do not want that so I have always been very strict about selecting what I do and don't do. That's one of the reasons I have always felt comfortable doing adverts for Pepsi. I have had a relationship with them since 2004. They have done a number of different adverts with big groups of footballers – doing battle with gladiators, surrounded by surf boards and huge waves, taking on tough-looking German supporters in the Fans' Park before the 2006 World Cup or as workmen setting up a sand pitch in the middle of the city, ready for a game.

I have met loads of fellow footballers but the truth is that the players who appear in a given advert don't always meet on the shoot. Fitting filming around a footballer's schedule is difficult; getting all the players together on the same day is virtually impossible. The first advert I did for Pepsi was filmed in Medinaceli, a medieval town in the province of Soria in northern Spain, about 200km from Madrid. I was just about the least well-known person there; ahead of me were stars like Beckham, Totti, Ronaldinho, Raúl and Roberto Carlos. I had such a small role in the scene that I hardly even got the chance to enjoy spending time with such big stars. The thing that most surprised me was that there were paparazzi hanging around the place. The company took precautions: we were driven from the hotel to the Plaza Mayor where the scene was being filmed and they had covered it over with sheets to make sure that no one saw the gladiators' costumes we wore. It was a huge production and I was there for the whole day. And all for a few seconds on screen.

Lots of the shoots have been done in Madrid. They created a beach complete with a swimming pool 'sea' in the aerodrome to film the surfing advert and the Fan Fest advert took us to a private sports club in Madrid where they set up a huge marquee for us to play in. Meanwhile, the advert where we appeared as workmen was filmed in Barcelona on a mock-up of a central street. It was the same players who had been together in Medinaceli, although we were also joined by Thierry Henry and Frank Lampard. It was good fun.

Ronaldinho arrived at one shoot having barely slept the night before because Barcelona had been celebrating winning the 2005 league title. I had to do some scenes with him and he was struggling, which was fair enough – after all, you don't win the league title every day.

I was also invited to the presentation of the advert along with Beckham and Roberto Carlos but this time it was my turn to struggle. During the press conference, I was having problems with gastroenteritis – an illness that seems to prey on me.

Off the pitch, David Beckham strikes me as a nice guy, polite and friendly. We couldn't talk to each other much during the Pepsi presentation because I wasn't well but I was taken by surprise: I had never personally witnessed the huge number of fans that follow him around. On the pitch, he has always been a great opponent and a good fellow professional. I swapped shirts with him and he struck me as a respectful and likeable person.

The beer company Mahou have also done a lot of adverts with footballers to help promote the Spanish league. One of the most famous was the one that was shot on a small concrete five-a-side pitch in the centre of Madrid. The theme was a series of challenge matches, first to two goals and winner stays on, against workers from different professions. The Mahou team was made up of Spanish internationals – Real Madrid goalkeeper Iker Casillas, Valencia midfielder Rubén Baraja, Valencia winger Joaquín, former Newcastle striker Albert Luque, who's now at Málaga, and me, Liverpool's No. 9. We played against a team of businessmen, waiters, airline pilots, bin men, and even the bride and groom from a wedding. The night before the shoot, I had barely slept. When they picked me up I felt terrible but I thought that the gastroenteritis – again! – would soon pass. It didn't. After the first few hours' shooting, I had to go and lie down while my colleagues had lunch. I was struggling so much that the final few scenes that night had to be filmed by a double. The director and the sponsor decided to send me home to rest. Luckily, the club had given us a couple of days off so I was fine by the time I had to go back to training.

One winter morning, there was a filming session for Kellogg's. They had done a number of scenes indoors but they decided that they needed to shoot some of the advert outside, so they chose a sports centre in the south of Madrid. It was two days before a Copa del Rey game with Atlético and after a morning session I left our training ground to head to the shoot with flu already starting to take hold.

Despite the blankets I was wrapped in and the fact that it was a short session, the cold cut right through me. I was frozen to the bone. By the time we'd finished I was sneezing and running a fever. I couldn't train the following day, but I did play the day after that. The score? 1–0; a goal from Torres, and Atlético through to the next round. It must have been the cereal bars that did it.

I recently started doing fashion shoots again after becoming the face of Emidio Tucci suits for Spain's biggest department store, El Corte Inglés. The shoot was done in Liverpool and I had to pose in the entire autumn 2008 and spring 2009 collection. I didn't always feel comfortable but there was a great team around me and the campaign was a huge success in Spain.

I have also collaborated with Aviva; with the international cosmetics company Puig Beauty & Fashion Group; with Pringles, who've also worked with other footballers; with Telepizza, the leading take-away and delivery company in Spain, for whom I had to dress up as an old man alongside my Spanish team-mate Carles Puyol; with Racer, one of the top five watchmaking companies in the world, who designed a Fernando Torres watch; with Toshiba, who have been at the head of Japan's industry for over a century; and with Cuatro TV, the television channel that broadcast Euro 2008 in Spain and who turned me into an all-powerful, football-playing robot.

Sometimes, doing ads has helped my friends too. One occasion was the campaign I did for Banco Gallego, a financial institution with a long history. They selected me because of my Galician roots – my father is from the north-west of Spain – and they asked me to choose three friends whose businesses I could promote through them. We produced adverts with a home-movie feel to give them authenticity: Nacho introducing his dog training school, Luis promoting tennis lessons for kids and adults, and Juan Carlos presenting his hairdressers. Apparently, their businesses have grown thanks to the publicity.

I've left one of my most important sponsors until last because they were the first to support me and have stayed with me ever since. My relationship with Nike goes back to the Nike Cup held in Italy in 1999, which was won by Atlético Madrid's Under-15s. I was named player of the tournament and part of the prize was a clothing contract with Nike. I have done countless adverts and photoshoots with them over almost ten years but three stand out more than the rest, one shocking, one funny and my favourite.

The shocking one was put together in a dark, bare photo studio in Madrid, after I had joined Liverpool. Nike chose five Spanish internationals who were set to play at Euro 2008: Puyol and Andres Iniesta from Barcelona, Cesc Fàbregas from

Arsenal, and Sergio Ramos from Real Madrid. With big marker pens, we covered our torsos with slogans – criticisms that Spanish fans had made of the national team in a poll, mistakes that they thought we'd made in the past, the historic stumbling blocks that prevented us from becoming champions. The idea was that we would learn from those and not fall into the same trap: this time we'd take it to the next level.

The one that was most fun was filmed on the streets of Madrid. I had to drive a yellow truck round the city with two Real Madrid players for passengers: Ramos and Cicinho, who's now at Roma. Once we had arrived at our destination we played a game in the street with three kids. Driving round with two 'enemies' was quite an experience.

But the best of the lot was the time that Nike turned Liverpool Spanish after I had arrived on Merseyside. In each scene, there was a Spanish touch: the famous silhouette of a Spanish bull alongside the road into the city, English school kids learning Spanish, red and yellow flags hanging from windows, people selling huge paella dishes down at the market, chip shops offering tapas, a workman climbing up to add an 'A' on the end of the legendary Cavern club to make it The 'Caverna', girls learning to dance flamenco … And all of it set to a Spanish version of the song the Kop dedicated me: 'Liverpool's No. 9'. The ending is brilliant. I walk through a park with my dog Llanta and a ball comes my way. When I kick it back to the lads playing football, one turns round and shouts back, 'Gracias, mate!'

XV

First Act: Chelsea at Anfield

'You're playing.' It's time for my debut at Anfield. And against Chelsea too. Sunday, 19 August. The second game of the Premier League season following the opening match against Aston Villa – a match we won thanks to a fantastic late Steven Gerrard free-kick.

I had played my first 78 minutes in England down in Birmingham, now it was time to play at Anfield for the first time. Rafa Benítez had called me into his office after delivering his morning team talk at Melwood on the day before the game. The truth is, I hadn't understood a word he said. It was hard enough to speak English, even harder in that situation when everyone is talking so quickly. That's why the coach wanted to speak to me individually. The first thing he told me was that I would be starting and that we would play with two strikers. He didn't tell me who my strike partner would be – I later found out that it was Dirk Kuyt – but he explained Chelsea's weaknesses to me, how José Mourinho's team functioned defensively and what position I had to take up when we didn't have the ball. It was a tactical lesson in my new team.

I kept a discreet silence when I left Rafa's office. I didn't say anything to anyone. The reason was simple: before the team meeting with Benítez that morning, Pepe Reina had told me that he thought I was going to be a substitute. He told me that the coach likes to rotate his players and that over the last few years Peter Crouch had played an important role whenever we faced Chelsea. His aerial game caused Chelsea lots of problems, which led him to believe that I would start my first Liverpool home game on the Anfield bench. I have to admit, I was a bit disappointed. Luckily, the disappointment didn't last much longer than half an hour.

My big day didn't start well. I left home for the stadium. When I started going round and round the streets, I realised that I was going the wrong way. I didn't recognise the buildings around me. Liverpool's players always have the choice of meeting at Anfield or fifteen minutes later at Melwood. It was a good job I always leave myself plenty of time, or else I would have been lost and late. I was driving through West Derby looking for signs to Anfield-Everton. But I took a turn too soon and I ended up on the wrong side of the stadium; I could see it down on the right. I would have to go all the way round the ground. As I sat at the traffic lights, a group of fans recognised me. So did the people setting up their stalls for the day, selling scarves and shirts. 'Good luck!' and 'Go out there and win!' they shouted. At least, that's what I think they shouted. I still take much the same route to the stadium on match days and the same people I saw that morning are always there, waiting to say hello and wish me well.

I was relaxed on the team bus. I sat at the back where there's a card table. I had Pepe Reina to my left and Xabi Alonso and Álvaro Arbeloa in front of me. We didn't talk about football; you end up talking about anything to kill the time and to ease the tension that a game like that always produces. Through the window, I could see that lots of fans were already wearing Liverpool shirts with my name and the No. 9 on the back. I had seen lots of fans in Switzerland and Holland wearing my shirt during pre-season but I didn't expect to see so many of them at Anfield. I was surprised: it seemed too soon for them to be backing such an unknown, someone who hadn't proved anything yet. Outside, the fans were already building up for the match and when we came off the bus they formed a passageway and cheered us as we made our way into the stadium.

I had been nice and relaxed the night before. That very week I had left the flat I had been staying at in the centre of the city and moved to a new rented house on the outskirts. The house was a mess: there were boxes half open all over the place, suitcases lying around, you couldn't find a thing. And as if to make it worse, every couple of minutes your ears took a hammering: the smoke alarm in the kitchen was really sensitive and seemed to go off every two minutes ... It was such a mess that I decided I couldn't be bothered to do any more, so I just sat on the sofa with the remote control and started channel hopping. I came across some WWF and decided to watch that because it was the only thing I could follow without understanding English. I wasn't thinking about Chelsea at all; I was in another world. I had so much to organize, so much to sort out, that I didn't even worry about the match, I didn't have time for nerves or excitement. I slept like a log until the bedroom was filled with sunlight. I never imagined dawn would come so early in Liverpool.

Not speaking English turned out to be an advantage at that stage. There were times when not knowing the language was a real problem but as a way of isolating yourself from everything it was fantastic. I didn't read the papers because I couldn't understand them, I didn't watch sports or news on television because I had no idea what was being said. I had no idea just how great the expectations surrounding me were. The only thing I understood were the things I was told in the dressing room and I didn't pay that much attention to them either. I was floating on a cloud. I didn't understand anything that was said to me. I felt like nothing bad could happen. I had no idea at all what awaited me that afternoon.

I soon found out. It was time to enjoy the moment. The only bad thing was the result: a draw that only happened because they were given a penalty that never was. The referee apologised for his mistake but it was too late. His decision had prevented it from being the perfect debut and we were left with a feeling of powerlessness; there is nothing you can do but watch an extraordinary result get snatched away. Despite the frustration of the draw, I went into the dressing room after the game feeling very positive. And feeling pleased with my decision to wear the same white boots that season – despite my sponsors Nike going ballistic with me.

Just before we went out onto the pitch, Reina looked at me and said: 'Enjoy it, you deserve it.' They had just finished singing 'You'll Never Walk Alone' and the atmosphere was spectacular. We wished each other luck and before I knew it the game was underway. I had a good chance early on. I wasted it but I was starting to get to know the way Gerrard plays. I knew that if I made a move, a dash to break away from my marker, he would see it. And so it proved. He played a long ball into the space on the left. I picked it up, came inside and ran towards the area. I thought about going on the outside but I saw John Terry. Tal Ben-Haim closed in, but gave me a metre. I stopped. So did he. I accelerated forward again, cutting inside, and slipped the shot into the far corner, to Petr Cech's left. The ball hit the post and ended up in the net.

Goal! My first goal at Anfield. I ran to the corner to celebrate … and found myself right in front of the Chelsea fans. I didn't even realise. I was used to away fans always being right up high, as they are in Spanish stadiums. No wonder my celebration was met with shouts and insults.

I hadn't thought about scoring because I hadn't really thought about the game. Of course I was looking forward to playing in one of the most intense and passionate games in England and of course I knew that it would be special against Chelsea. When I arrived at the stadium, I went straight into the dressing room. I didn't go out to have a look at the pitch or see what condition the grass was in. I just sat there flicking through the programme that someone had left on the bench and busied myself filling an envelope with tickets for my family and friends who had come to share my first game at Anfield with me. Five minutes before we went out, Benítez spoke to us again. It's a moment for psychology rather than tactics. He reminded us of how strong Chelsea were – they had been Premier League champions for the previous two seasons – and how important it was to pick up points against a direct rival. He also told us what it would mean to the fans to win. I didn't need a translator to understand what it meant for the team; I could see how committed they were. I did, though, make a mental note to get on with my English.

As I was getting changed my feet felt cold, so I put sports socks on top of my Liverpool socks, before putting tape around my ankles. It's become a custom now, both for Liverpool and Spain. I don't think I'll ever go back to just wearing football socks.

When I had time to look back on the game and reflect on it, it dawned on me just how different the game is in England. Goals would help but I knew that I was a long way behind my team-mates. I knew I would have to work really hard. Without that effort I knew that success was impossible. The tactical discipline of teams in England was not as strict as I had been used to in Spain. Teams played more with their hearts in England, the commitment was greater, everyone pushed themselves to the very limit. Tactics were less important than the physical side of the game; the small details mattered less. I still had time to adapt and I knew that I would get better bit by bit but I also knew I would have to get used to it quickly. English football is fantastic – it's up and down, there is no time to rest. It's harder but more exciting for the fans.

I got home to find the same mess I had left behind. Suitcases with clothes hanging out, boxes half unpacked, things in the wrong place, junk everywhere. What was I expecting? For the goal to have worked a miracle? For me, somehow, to come home to a house where everything was in order? There was an important price to pay for the mess, too: I gave the shirt I wore on my debut against Aston Villa to my brother Israel and I've found the one I wore on my Champions League debut against Toulouse, but the one I wore that day against Chelsea has disappeared. My first goal, my first game at Anfield. I've looked for it everywhere and can't find it. The mess of my new home swallowed it up, never to be seen again.

XVI
The best league in the world

It wasn't the best goal I've scored in the Premier League but it was the one I most enjoyed – because of where it was, because of who our opponents were, because of what it meant.

It came at Old Trafford against Manchester United, with the league title at stake. There was no room for error. If we lost that morning we knew that we would wave goodbye to our slim chances of staying in the fight for the title. The omens weren't good. We didn't need reminding that we hadn't won at Old Trafford for a long time. I couldn't get the previous season's 3–0 defeat out of my head. And on top of all that we started in the worst possible way. A penalty opened the scoring for Manchester United.

But then, out of nothing, Nemanja Vidić hesitated on a long clearance from Martin Skrtel. I battled for the ball, beat him to it and found myself one on one with Edwin Van der Sar to score the equaliser and spark a comeback and a fantastic team performance. Steven Gerrard, Fabio Aurelio and Andrea Dossena scored to give us real hope of winning a title that we had chased for almost twenty years. Our fans went wild; it was the perfect end to a special week in which we had beaten Real Madrid 4–0 at Anfield. We had defeated our biggest rivals 4–1 away from home. The fans could have kept singing until the following morning.

It wasn't so long ago that I made my debut in the Premier League, a competition I had wanted to experience for a long time. Ironically, just like my debut for Spain I made my bow dressed in white, the colours of Atlético's rivals Real Madrid. Liverpool were facing Aston Villa at Villa Park. I look back on it as a difficult match that I struggled to get into. A tough ground to visit, with fans right on top of you and played at a frenetic pace. The atmosphere was fantastic and it was a great introduction to the intensity of the English game. A wonderful free-kick from Steven Gerrard in the final few minutes gave us victory. I had arrived in the Premier League.

The Premier League is better organised than La Liga; it is similar in feel to the Champions League. Less rigid, perhaps, but very serious: the stadiums are full, the pitches are perfect and there is a real intensity about it. It didn't disappoint me at all. In fact, it was better than I could have imagined, the kind of league you love to play in: your efforts are rewarded, the fans really respect you and get behind you. No wonder every footballer wants to experience it. It's fantastic. It is the most attractive league in the world, with a global audience and a real presence in every country. It's a sign of its strength that the Big Four dominate in Europe. The emergence of Barcelona might have put the brakes on English dominance a bit but the Premier League still boasted three of the four Champions League semi-finalists in 2008. A few years ago, Italy was recognised as the strongest league in Europe, then it was Spain but now England has the best league. Every player is attracted to the Premier League.

The way the league is set up for fans makes an occasion of every game. Fans go to the games to enjoy themselves and have a fun day. There's a real respect towards the players. Even if you play badly, the fans are grateful for the effort and don't get on your back. There is no fierce criticism, whinging or complaints. The atmosphere is perfect. There are times when it reminds me more of the atmosphere you get at World Cups and European Championships than league games in Spain. When it comes to the football itself, it's even better.

The Premier League can be summed up in a few words: intensity, speed, and nobility. Everyone tries to win; there's no sitting back. It's perfect for me: the Premier League fits my game like a glove. I could hardly enjoy myself more. It's just right.

A BRITISH NEWSPAPER SUMMED IT UP IN AN ARTICLE PUBLISHED IN JUNE 2008:

1 *Torres is the debutant with the best goal-scoring average in over a hundred years of history at Liverpool. With a goal every 1.36 games he has overtaken Liverpool legends like John Aldridge (a goal every 1.55 games), Ian Rush (1.63), Roger Hunt (1.65), Robbie Fowler (1.83), Michael Owen (1.91) and Kenny Dalglish (2).*

2 *He finished second in the Premier League top scorers' chart on 24, level with Adebayor. Only the European Golden Boot winner Cristiano Ronaldo, with 31, finished ahead of Torres.*

3 *With 24 goals, he is the most prolific foreign debutant in the history of the Premier League, overtaking Ruud Van Nistelrooy, who scored 23 in the 2001–02 season.*

4 *A goal every 106 minutes makes him the second most effective goalscorer in the Premier League. Only Cristiano Ronaldo boasts a better record with a goal every 89.48 minutes, and Torres is a long way ahead of Adebayor (a goal every 123.08 for Arsenal), Roque Santa Cruz (169.21, at Blackburn Rovers), Berbatov (201.06, at Tottenham) and Keane (182.60, at Tottenham).*

5 *Torres's 33 goals in all competitions completes the best season from a Liverpool player this century. Michael Owen held the previous best record with 28 goals in 2002–03. Fernando has raised the bar. He is also the first Liverpool player since Robbie Fowler to score more than twenty league goals in a season.*

6 The Madrileño has become the first Liverpool player in history to score in eight consecutive top–flight games at Anfield. Only Roger Hunt can equal that figure, but he did so in 1961–62, when Liverpool were playing in the second division.

7 Torres is the first player to score back to back Anfield hat-tricks since 1946. Jake Balmer was the last man to achieve that feat at Liverpool's fortress. 61 years later, Torres matched his record and entered into the annals of Liverpool legend.

8 Only three Premiership teams have managed to prevent Torres from scoring against them this season: Manchester United, Aston Villa and Birmingham.

9 Torres ended Rafa Benítez's terrible run at Stamford Bridge. Not since 30 April last year had the Merseyside team managed to score against Chelsea under Rafa Benítez. Torres did so in the Champions League semi-final second leg.

10 Voted for by his fellow professionals, the PFA included him in their team of the season. He was also named the Premierships's second-best player for 2007–08 at the Football Writers' awards, the first time in 61 years (since 1947) that a Spaniard finished in the top three. He also finished second in the Liverpool fans' player of the year poll for 2007, despite having only been at the club for five months. And he was the Premiership's player of the month for February.

I was confident that I would have a good first season but things went even better than I could have ever imagined. The only thing that was missing was a title at the end of it. To be able to adapt to English football so quickly and win over my team-mates and fans so soon was incredible. I've felt loved from the very first day. The challenge now is to be able to maintain that level and not let people down. The expectations are high now; I have to be equal to them. I'm aware that the fans will support me whatever I do but that at the same time they demand the best from me. That makes me feel proud. Just as it makes me feel proud when people remind me what I have achieved in the short time I have been in England.

All of which leaves me open mouthed and a little embarrassed. I have had two intense years. Looking back, if the first season stood out for the hat-tricks, the thing I remember most fondly about the second are the goals I scored in key games.

In 2007–08, I scored hat-tricks in consecutive games against Middlesbrough and West Ham at Anfield. They were unforgettable moments and a new experience too. I had never scored a hat-trick for Atlético Madrid, the only time I had scored three in a single match was for Spain against San Marino.

The match against Boro – which I ended on the bench – didn't start well, either. We fell behind but we managed to turn the game round and win. When the referee blew the final whistle I went up to him to ask for the match ball. He told me that he would give it to me when we got to the dressing room but the fans started booing him and in the end he was forced to hand it over to me there and then. In the following match, which I also finished on the bench, it was Gerrard who went up to the referee to ask for the ball. He then handed it to me and it was passed round the dressing room for my team-mates to sign. Both balls take pride of place at home – two 'trophies' I treasure. Against West Ham, I hit the post before I'd scored the third and I could feel the disappointment from the fans. They were even more determined than me to get a second consecutive hat-trick. Fortunately, I had another chance which didn't go to waste. I look back on the first of my three hat-tricks that season fondly, too, in the Carling Cup at Reading in a 4–2 win. But I wouldn't swap it for the Anfield ones.

In 2008–09 I managed to score twice in each of five matches. In one of them, I got what I consider to be the best goal I have scored in a Liverpool shirt. It came against Blackburn Rovers.

I got a long ball from Jamie Carragher near the top right corner of the penalty area, controlled it on my chest, pulled away from the defender, saw the goalkeeper slightly off his line, turned and, on the bounce, sent it over him and into the far corner. Luckily, it came off perfectly.

I also scored two against Chelsea at Anfield, in the dying minutes of the match. Time was ticking away, it was 0–0 and we just couldn't get the goal. Then, suddenly, we got the breakthrough that enabled us to keep fighting it out with Manchester United for the league title. It was an important brace for me because I had just come back from an injury and to get two against such difficult opponents gave me confidence and a morale boost after a hard year. The third brace I got at Anfield was against Arsenal in a crazy 4–4 draw. It's not exactly normal for Liverpool to concede eight in a week – we'd just drawn 4–4 with Chelsea in the Champions League too – and it was an incredible end-to-end match. In the final analysis though, the draw was worthless to us and left a bad taste in my mouth. That was the night the league slipped away from us.

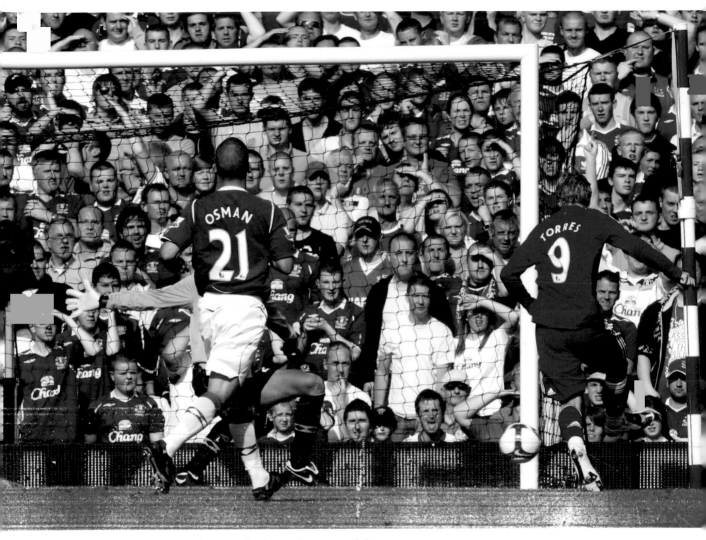

Scoring at Goodison Park always has a special taste.
That day against Everton, I got two.

The other two matches I scored twice in were at Goodison Park in the derby against Everton and against Manchester City at Eastlands. We were losing 2–0 but we fought back and Dirk Kuyt got the winner late on. It was a great victory against difficult opponents. Against Everton, the referee disallowed a goal that would have given me a hat-trick. He blew for a 'foul' by Kuyt that wasn't and my third of the afternoon was wiped out. The two I did get came in the 59th and 63rd minutes and were the first goals I had scored at Goodison because the season before I had missed the game through injury. The Liverpool fans gave me an incredible ovation.

Everyone in the team knows just how much the fans want to win the league. It's been almost twenty years now. We know that winning back the trophy that means the most to our fans is the key challenge ahead of us now.

We have to claw back our record as the team with the most English league titles. We're still England's most successful club when it comes to the European Cup but we know that we also have to become the No. 1 side domestically once again. Injuries cost us dear in 2008–09, despite getting the better of both Manchester United and Chelsea over the course of the season: we won at Stamford Bridge and Old Trafford. In the end, we probably lost out on the league because of the points that slipped away at Anfield. We drew too many times at home.

When it comes to centre-back pairings, my toughest opponents have been John Terry and Ricardo Carvalho, and Rio Ferdinand and Nemanja Vidić. They are two formidable partnerships. I know that a lot has been said about my confrontations with Terry but they have never gone beyond an honourable battle on the pitch. That's normal between two competitive players and has never spilled over into anything else. Chelsea's centre-backs complement each other perfectly – they're strong, aggressive and very quick. There's little to choose between them and United's pair. Ferdinand and Vidić are colossal in the air but that doesn't mean they lack anything when it comes to anticipation and positioning. They hold the line very well, even with two attacking full-backs alongside them who always want to get forward. Chelsea and United have chosen different ways of setting up their defensive barriers, but both are extremely hard to overcome. You have to be at your very best against them.

And then there are the goalkeepers. I'm lucky: the best goalkeeper in the Premier League plays for my team. Having Pepe Reina on my side is a relief. I'd also like to highlight the work that Liverpool's Brazilian goalkeeper Diego Cavalieri does. He's an exceptional goalkeeper. As for the opposition, the hardest to beat are Petr Cech, who is fantastic, and Shay Given. I haven't been able to score against him for Newcastle or Manchester City. He's got the beating of me so far. But hopefully I'll be able to put that right soon.

XVII

My
Champions
League bow

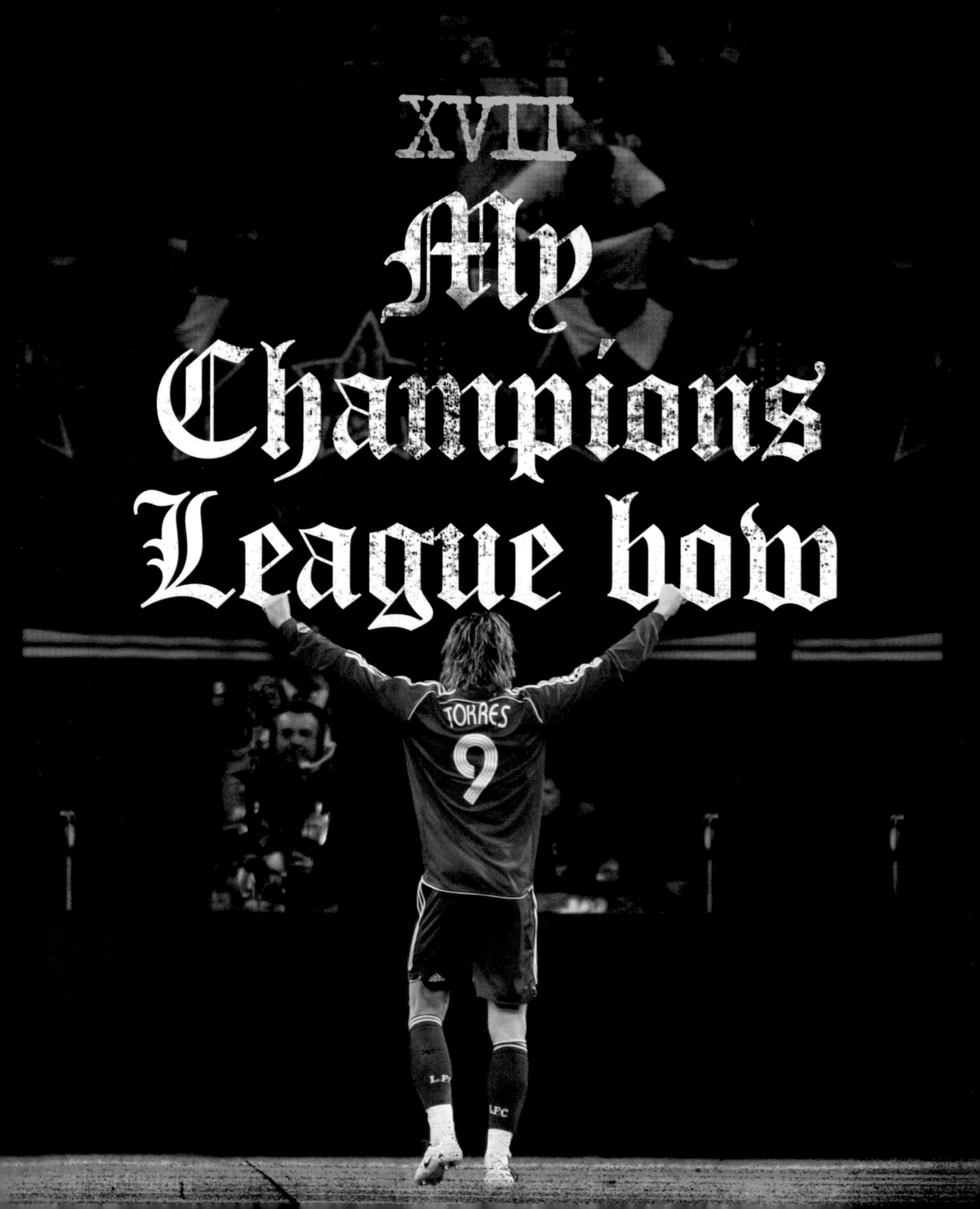

Through the window of the team
bus the stadium struck me.
My Champions League dream
really came true at the San Siro.
It's an incredible place and one
that surprised me: the facilities,
the stands, the atmosphere,
everything about it is wonderful …
playing there for the first time
and scoring was the perfect way
to end years of waiting for the
chance to appear in Europe's
biggest club competition.

Jamie Carragher had told me about the draw one day after training at Melwood. Inter were difficult opponents, footballing aristocrats, and they had the advantage of playing the second leg at home. But Liverpool took the draw in their stride: no one was scared and no one was overexcited either. It was February 2008 and the match at Anfield was a slow, cautious affair against a well-organised team that sat back and waited for us, satisfied with a 0-0 draw and happy to wait for the chance to catch us with a dead ball or a set play – all the more so after the sending off of Marco Materazzi. But we showed great patience and they couldn't tilt the tie their way. Instead, we secured an impressive victory.

I was involved in Materazzi getting sent off. Twice, long balls were played over the back of the Italian defence. Both times, I beat him for pace, got behind him and was brought down. Marco got a yellow card both times. Both of them were a little harsh in my opinion, certainly by Premier League standards. But then this was the Champions League and the refereeing is stricter. The referee judged both challenges to be dangerous and worthy of a card, while Materazzi thought it was worth taking the risk with the second tackle because he considered it virtually impossible for a referee to take out two cards in such quick succession. He was wrong. As the game developed we kept up the pressure until the end and it was in the final minutes that we finally got the goals, through Dirk Kuyt and Steven Gerrard. Dirk's goal left us very happy and holding on to an important lead but we felt we had deserved more and that it still wasn't enough; when Steven scored, we knew we would travel to Milan with the tie where we wanted it.

Not that it was easy in Italy. Inter had more chances, and clearer ones too. Pepe Reina kept us alive. Burdisso's sending off tipped the balance in our favour and on the counter-attack I took a shot from outside the area that beat Julio César. There was only one thing left to do: hand my shirt to Demetrio Albertini, a former team-mate of mine at Atlético Madrid and now a huge Milan fan, having previously played for the club for many years.

The Champions League campaign had begun in Porto back in September 2007. I'd been waiting for so long! I was more excited about the second match, which would be my first at Anfield, against Olympique de Marseille – a game we lost – but destiny wanted me to make my bow in Portugal, a country that's been important to me during my career. It was in Portugal that I made my debut for the Spanish national team and now I was making my Champions League debut there too. We were facing a side that knew exactly what the competition was all about. In the group phase it's important to get on the right track from the start, so a draw wasn't a bad result for us. Porto were the better side, they took the lead and dominated the majority of the match. But Liverpool's status began to impose itself on the game. Or at least on me; it was a match in which I discovered that Liverpool really are great. Kuyt's goal allowed us to come out of the match alive and showed me that when things get tough, Liverpool unite, defend well, and ride out the storm. We found ourselves down to ten men after Jermaine Pennant got sent off and still took a point home. It was a bittersweet debut because we didn't win and I didn't score but we were happy considering the way the match had gone.

Porto were again the opponents when I experienced my first really big European night at Anfield. After a group phase full of ups and downs, we went into the last two matches knowing that we had to win them both: at home against Porto and away to Marseilles. With no room for error, we needed six points from six. The match against Porto was exactly the same as the first clash, only with the boot on the other foot. We dominated the game. My first Champions League goal came from a Steven Gerrard corner. It was a move we'd practised to take advantage of their zonal marking system – I got behind Lucho González and, all alone, headed in. The problem was that we couldn't turn our domination into more goals and they equalised.

That was one of the reasons why I wanted to depart Atlético; getting the chance to play in the Champions League was key to me leaving Madrid.

A draw would have seen us go out and time was slipping away until, driven on by the Anfield roar, substitute Harry Kewell sent a ball through for me. I battled with José Bosingwa, got one on one with the goalkeeper and put us into the lead. We were 2–1 up and I had got my first two European goals. Soon Gerrard and Crouch added two more to round off the night. The atmosphere was incredible – and different to the atmosphere in Premier League games. At night there's something special about the way the fans push you on.

I had dreamt of nights like that for so long. At the age of 23, I still hadn't played in Europe.

Competing for the Champions League was my goal and signing for Liverpool helped me chase it. In three years they had reached two finals and won the tournament. When I signed, Liverpool were even better equipped to win in Europe than at home.

The Champions League is a fantastic tournament to watch on television and to play in. There is a special feeling that surrounds every Champions League match; there's a kind of magic in the air; from the tournament's hymn to the fight to succeed amongst the world's best players and its biggest clubs. It's watched all over the world and every player wants to be involved. If you don't play in the Champions League it's as if you don't exist. No matter what you do in your domestic league, it doesn't seem to matter without the Champions League. It's the biggest club competition there is and it's there that players really prove their worth. If you don't play in it, you can't prove how good you are. If you're fighting it out for the Champions League, your status grows. If you're not, you're going backwards. Week after week, it is the stage for the finest footballers.

When I at last made my debut it was exactly as I had expected it to be: the organisation is like a World Cup or European Championship. Every little detail is taken care of, there is no room for mistakes. With each instruction handed out by Uefa's delegates, the seriousness and importance of the competition is brought home.

We began the tournament with the qualifier against Toulouse. At that stage, the games don't count as official Champions League matches. There are no stars on the shirt, no hymn before the match. When the draw was made I was surprised: Toulouse struck me as a dangerous opponent and I was worried about not getting through, yet my team-mates seemed extremely relaxed. They weren't over-confident but they knew we'd get through comfortably. They were right: we won both games without the result ever being in much doubt. They knew what playing for Liverpool meant on the continent; I didn't yet. In France, I found out just how much weight the Liverpool shirt carries. It was time to stop worrying about our opponents.

We soon returned to France, this time to face Olympique Marseilles, the same team that had ruined my Champions League debut at Anfield. I don't remember how many it was but I know that Liverpool had gone a huge number of games without losing at home, but a great goal from Mathieu Valbuena ended that run. Benfica had been the last team to win at Anfield and knock the Reds out. Now, going into Match Day 3, we were in a difficult position again. We had picked up just one point from six and we still had to travel to Turkey – a trip to 'Hell' awaited us. We had to win in Marseilles's Vélodrome. Just before the match, my mind was cast back to how furious I had been after the first game with them, when we had lost 1–0 at Anfield. We hadn't played well that day, it's true, but nor did we deserve to lose. It was time to put it right. And I was convinced that we would do just that.

Marseilles's fans create a really hostile atmosphere but we silenced them quickly. After ten minutes we were already 2–0 up and had the game under control. Just as they started to push their way back into the game we got the third, then a fourth. A lot has been said about the goal I got. It was even voted goal of the season in Europe by Liverpool's fans. Individual goals are often the most striking and skilful but I don't think they're the most beautiful. At the time, sure I was delighted, but quite honestly I preferred one I scored a few months later.

Although we surrendered to Besiktas in Istanbul, we made up for that by producing a historic performance in the second game against them. The same players who had been beaten in Turkey hammered them 8–0 in Liverpool. I watched the match from the bench at Anfield and it was unforgettable. Besiktas had hurt Liverpool's pride and they paid for it.

The team I least wanted to face next was Arsenal, mainly because I know that when you play them you spend a lot of the time chasing shadows. There isn't a team in the world, except perhaps Barcelona, that keeps the ball as long as they do.

But Arsenal it was and the tie started badly when we conceded from a set play. Luckily, Kuyt quickly equalised. That was the prelude for a second half when we suffered more than we should have done. It finished 1–1 in London and the second leg was at Anfield but I was swamped by doubts. I didn't know if playing the second leg at home is such an advantage. It would be every bit as hard as it had been at the Emirates. For the first twenty minutes we didn't even see the ball and Abou Diaby gave them the lead but we were lucky: Sami Hyypiä equalised quickly.

Until then the best goal I had scored in the tournament was the one in Marseilles. But the one I scored that night against Arsenal to put us back in the lead had it all. It's my favourite, for the way the stadium erupted, for the noise in the ground, for the way the fans screamed and cheered. Peter Crouch flicked the ball on, I turned Philippe Senderos, carried the ball half a metre, steadied myself and finished. Words fail me when it comes to describing the reaction of the fans. We'd done it. Or so it seemed. Instead, there was more suffering to come. On an absurd counter-attack that we should never have let happen, Theo Walcott brilliantly set up

Emanuel Adebayor to score. There were seven minutes left and everything was in tatters. There wasn't time for another comeback. Only there was: as usual, Anfield's magic was contagious. The passion of the fans, the roar and the belief coming from stands carried us forward and Ryan Babel was the hero, winning a penalty which made it 3–2, and scoring a fourth goal. It was the perfect end to an incredible night. Another European night at Anfield. The night I had dreamed of for so long.

My first European adventure came to a close with what has become a Champions League classic in recent years: Liverpool versus Chelsea. In the two previous semi-finals between the sides a single goal had been enough to tip the balance. Every little detail would be vital if we were to book our ticket to the final in Moscow. And, sadly, so it proved: one little detail was enough to deny us the chance to reach the final. At Anfield Kuyt's goal led to a tight, tactical game. We were strong at the back and the game went exactly the way we had planned … until additional time at the end of the 90 minutes, when an own goal gave us an uphill task. John Arne Riise's moment of misfortune sent us to Stamford Bridge with a dangerous 1–1 draw. It was also a huge psychological blow.

The 90 minutes at Stamford Bridge were similar to the 90 we'd played at Anfield. Didier Drogba's goal gave them the lead but we were still only a single goal from keeping the tie alive. Yossi Benayoun played the ball through and I beat Petr Cech to send the game into extra-time. We had half an hour more to find a winner but we let our guard slip and suffered another moment of bad luck. Hyypiä didn't see Michael Ballack coming across him and gave away a penalty. The goal meant we had to chase the game, we lost our shape and they added a third with a great move. By then, I was already on the bench. I hadn't expected to be taken off but I had a few muscle problems and Benítez didn't want to take any risks. The final slipped through our fingers. It would have been incredible to finish my first-ever Champions League campaign by climbing to the summit but it wasn't to be. It was an incredible experience. There had been great games and great goals. The final would have to wait. I had to leave something for future campaigns.

XVIII
Meeting in Madrid

It felt like I had been shot.
A sharp, sudden pain went
through my leg. I knew immediately
what had happened and I also
knew what it meant. I knew that
I could forget about returning to the
Vicente Calderón to face Atlético
Madrid in the Champions League.
That was all I could think about.

It happened in Brussels during a World Cup qualifier for Spain against Belgium and it was the second time in that 2008–09 season I had torn the same muscle. My hamstring had exploded again. I knew it was serious; I knew it was more than just a pulled muscle or a strain. I was inconsolable. I realised that I might not even make it for the return match against Atlético at Anfield. Just how much I was missing out on quickly dawned on me. I arrived in the dressing room upset, angry and in pain.

Once I had showered, the worry took over. I started to wonder if I had picked up a serious injury that would keep me out for a long time. I had a bad feeling about it. I had enjoyed good times in Brussels with the national team; now I was experiencing the other side of the coin. I had scored twice there to leave us in a strong position to qualify for the 2006 World Cup; now I was heading for the dressing room with a torn muscle barely a third of the way through the first half. The few minutes I had played until then had offered no warning. I felt fine, the injury seemed to have healed perfectly. I risked a sprint because I didn't feel the slightest pain … but the muscle disagreed and decided it had had enough.

As the days passed, so my fears were confirmed. The prognosis of three weeks without playing turned out to be optimistic. Muscle injuries are always hard to call. You have to judge by the way you are feeling day to day. I knew that it would be a slow process to heal and that rushing it would only lead me to taking unwise risks. I would have to be satisfied with becoming a spectator when the two teams that have marked my football career came face to face. Bit by bit, my hopes of playing at Anfield dissolved.

I had heard the draw over the phone. Margarita Garay had handed me the phone and a good friend of mine, an Atléti supporter, was on the other end. The first call came through: 'Marseilles–PSV'.

'Atlético?' I asked.

'Nothing yet.'

Then Atlético came out. The phone rang but I didn't reach it first time. When I did, the voice said: 'Liverpool have got Atlético.'

'Seriously?' I asked.

'I'm not joking,' came the reply, 'and I don't find it remotely funny.'

'Well,' I joked, 'we're going to beat you.'

I was happy: Atlético were the team I wanted. I would have preferred to play them later on, not in the group stage, but at least this way we could both go through. I was really excited about the chance to experience such a special moment. I was going back to Madrid. I was going home.

We both started the group well, with Liverpool beating Olympique de Marseille. Winning at the Vélodrome two years running, as Liverpool did, isn't easy. At that stage, Atlético Madrid were an unknown quantity in the Champions League and hadn't played in the competition since 1996 and yet they started excellently: they defeated PSV 3–0 in Eindhoven, immediately making a case to be considered favourites to get through the group.

The injury prevented me from even travelling to Madrid. Atlético invited me to watch the match as their guest but I didn't want to be the centre of attention. I really appreciated the gesture but, after speaking with Rafa Benítez and the medical staff at Liverpool, I decided that the best thing to do was to stay in England and continue with my treatment at Melwood, so I ended up watching the game at home on television.

During the game I heard the Liverpool fans sing my song a number of times and the final score – a 1–1 draw – added to the sense of brotherhood between two sets of fans who'd already been united by having me in common. Liverpool's fans created a special atmosphere and their example proved contagious. It was the perfect marriage. The connection between Atlético and Liverpool fans was incredible – and was symbolised by them swapping scarves and shirts.

' The happiest moment of the season for me came when both sets of fans joined forces to chant my name together. It was a really emotional moment. I couldn't believe it. The sadness I felt at not being able to play and the disappointment at not even being able to be there at the Calderón were overtaken by the joy I felt at the friendship shown by the two sets of fans. There's no doubt that Atlético's fans still see me as one of them and that Liverpool's fans understand that. '

Destiny had reserved another pleasant surprise for me. Despite the speculation, I knew that it was impossible for me to be fit in time to play the second leg. My injury was getting better but things were progressing more slowly than we had hoped and it still didn't feel right. Because of the risks involved in playing, it was best to be prudent. But this time I was able to go to the ground to watch the match live and when I arrived at Anfield, I passed by the Atlético end and they started to cheer and sing my name. I felt that the applause was warm and sincere; the welcome they gave me was heartfelt. I thanked them and headed to the dressing room, where I came across some of the Atlético players, like Kun Aguero, Leo Franco and Maxi Rodríguez, as well as Ignacio Ambriz and Miguel Bastón, who were part of the coaching staff. Javier Aguirre, the coach, was suspended and wasn't allowed in the dressing room area. I was surprised how relaxed Kun was. 'Aren't you going to get changed?' I asked. 'I'm sub,' he replied with a smile. A strange feeling washed over me. I had crossed over to the other side, but not entirely. I wanted Liverpool to win and yet I didn't want Atlético to lose.

Of course, it was a completely different story when we faced Real Madrid. I was training on my own with one of the physios when one of the guys from the press department, Steve, came over and told us that we would be facing Real Madrid. I smiled and told him they were exactly the team I wanted to face. I had spent ages telling Pepe Reina and Álvaro Arbeloa: 'We're going to get Madrid and we're going to beat them.' I was convinced on both scores. I fancied playing them for a lot of reasons: being an *atlético* means that every time I face Madrid it is special, Madrid had never played at Anfield in their history and when the draw was made we were playing really well and they were struggling. Two months later, though, the situation had changed completely. Picking a favourite was impossible.

I was surprised by the lack of prudence shown by Real Madrid's president in the days leading up to the game. While players like Raúl, Guti and Casillas were cautious in the things they said, the remarks made by their president Vicente Boluda could not have been more different. He claimed Madrid would hammer us.

The Spanish media followed his lead and the feeling we got was that they thought Madrid would go through comfortably. It was as if Liverpool's history counted for nothing. I thought that they – and I want to reiterate that by 'they' I don't mean the club's players – showed a lack of respect towards Liverpool.

It was the first time I had been to Spain to appear in a competitive match as a Liverpool player. There was a really special, passionate atmosphere around the match. Maybe the non-Spaniards amongst the Liverpool players took it in their stride more, maybe they were more laid back about it, but I could really feel something in the air. I approached it like a derby. The truth is, though, that when I went out onto the pitch at the Santiago Bernabéu the reception wasn't as hostile as I had expected. Maybe my goal for Spain in Vienna had won some Madrid fans over to my side, however much club football still takes precedence over the national team.

The match started badly. I sprained my ankle in the first move of the game. I was battling with Pepe, he put the brakes on and as I tried to do the same, my ankle twisted. I thought it was nothing but twenty minutes later I could see that it was swollen. I asked the physios to change the strapping on it to increase the support and also give me a painkilling injection. I had to take the scissors to my boot and cut it open to be able to get it back on again. At half time, Rafa Benítez asked me how it was and, after having the injection, I told him it was fine. But fifteen minutes into the second half he decided to take me off. I saw Yossi Benayoun's goal from the bench – and as the ball hit the net, my pain disappeared. The journey home, on the other hand, was hell. I was in agony and could hardly walk. Even the orthopaedic boot I was wearing didn't seem to make any difference.

I pushed hard to speed up my recovery and although it was a risk I asked to be included in the team for the second leg. The Spanish media were still saying that Madrid's history, their size as a club, would be enough to carry them to victory in the second leg. There were comments made by Madrid's coaching staff too. In Spain, they tried to explain our victory at the Bernabéu by accusing us of having been boring and defensive, which surprised us. It also gave us a little added motivation. During the warm up, I felt dreadful. I looked at my ankle and could no longer do anything except just hope it held up. I took a painkiller before kick-off but still didn't feel comfortable. There was nothing for it: I had to grit my teeth and get on with it.

We got into the game very quickly. We could hardly have played better in the first half. It was superb. The fans got behind us and we went for it. We really pushed and Madrid just couldn't handle it. It was a brilliant victory. My goal was just one moment in a match in which our superiority and spirit was evident from the very start. We showed an incredible desire to roll over them and did just that. Over the course of the tie, we beat Madrid in two different ways: in the first leg we beat them by displaying tactical control, while in the second leg we beat them with an extraordinary display of attacking football. At the end of the match, Raúl once again showed his class and the elegance with which he represents Real Madrid by looking for me to offer his congratulations. He always shows great humility and respect and he never hides on or off the pitch. He is an example to us all.

After defeating Real Madrid, we had to face Chelsea. Yet again. It was another tactical match but this time we weren't good enough. They were easily the better side at Anfield. We weren't ourselves; we weren't Liverpool. And that's despite the fact that the game started so well for us when I got the opening goal. The mistakes racked up and we went into the second leg 3–1 down. It was a scoreline we never expected. And when we should have been at our most calm – after scoring – we instead became nervous and out of control, even if we did show that you always have to have faith. The 4–4 draw at Stamford Bridge was a memorable match that proved once again that Liverpool are a special club with a great history. We had fallen with honour. It had seemed impossible but we had been very, very close to pulling it off twice: at 2–0 up and when we went to 3–3 then to 4–3 up in the couple of minutes towards the end, before they made it 4–4, and 7–5 on aggregate. We left with our heads held high having done justice to the red shirt. The ovation we received the following day when we arrived at the memorial service for the victims of Hillsborough will stay with me forever.

XIX

Fortress Melwood

The truth is, I was too embarrassed to approach Diego Maradona. Really. Javier Mascherano had told us that the Argentina legend was going to visit Liverpool's Melwood training ground to speak to Rafa Benítez and have a look around. The excitement it caused couldn't have been any greater if a film star had turned up. Normally Melwood is a model of quiet serenity. Not that day. I'd never seen it like it.

I was in the physios' room getting treatment for a muscle injury and people kept coming in, babbling excitedly about their encounter with Diego Maradona after having photographs taken with him. All the staff, first team players, reserves … everyone had dropped by the manager's office to meet El Diego and ask for an autograph or a photo. Everyone except me. When I finished my session, I went up to the manager's office to join the queue but when I got there I found myself alone and the door shut. I heard a noise from the floor below and went to have a look. There, in the entrance to Melwood, Maradona was saying goodbye to the last few people to grab him for a photo. A feeling of respect, a kind of awe, came over me; I didn't want to approach him. I didn't dare. It was enough for me to see him there, barely ten metres away.

But then that is Maradona. I never saw him play live and didn't see him at Mexico '86 or Italia '90 but I did watch him on television at the World Cup in the USA in 1994. Beyond the legend that now surrounds him is someone born into poverty but with an extraordinary talent for playing football. He touched heaven and hell. Every side of football is present in him, from the greatest imaginable successes to the greatest possible failures. The world that surrounds football is something that we all have to get used to. Every player suddenly finds that he is surrounded by new friends who appear and disappear again depending on what they can get out of you. Being Maradona can't be easy: everybody is on top of you, everyone talks about you and judges you, you don't have the slightest opportunity to turn off. Society has never allowed him the escape or relief that I imagine he must need at times. That serves as a warning for all professional sportsmen.

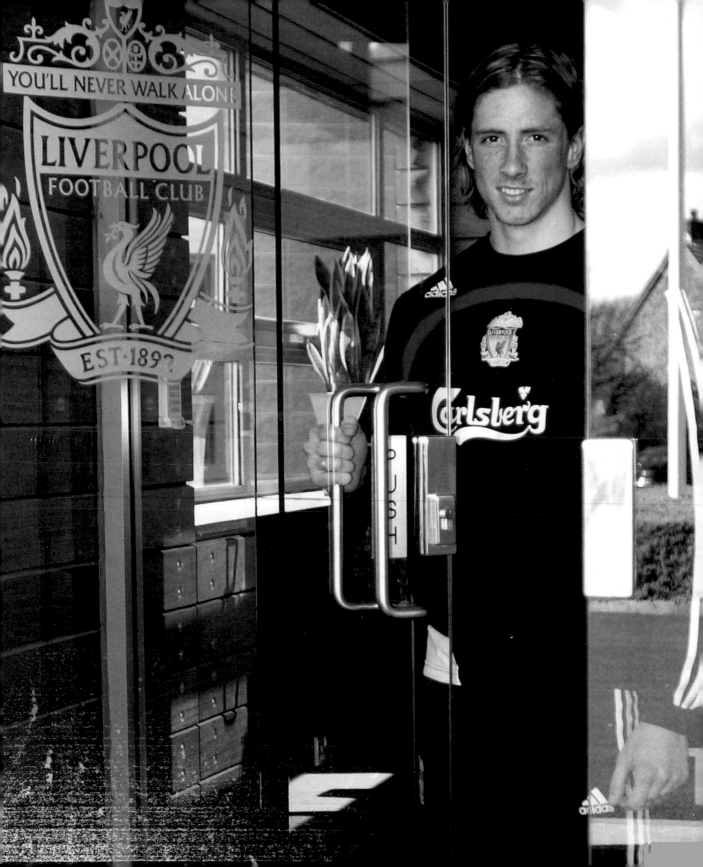

Melwood has all the space and state-of-the-art facilities a player needs to work; you have everything you could ask for at your fingertips. For a footballer, it's the perfect working environment. But the thing that I really like about it is sharing every day with the staff there. Working alongside loyal, faithful people committed to the cause, people who suffer when things are going badly for Liverpool and enjoy life when things are going well, is a lesson in humility. It brings you closer to the way fans feel and helps you keep your feet on the ground. I learnt all their names in a month. I felt like I had been transported back to when I was at Atlético and I used to go and visit the staff in the offices at the Vicente Calderón once a week. I was lucky to be able to count lots of the people who worked for Atléti amongst my friends.

It was those friends – people like Briñas, Angelines, Chacón, Charo, Arturo and Bustamente – who showed me what Atlético meant off the pitch, who revealed the idiosyncrasies of a club that's over a hundred years old. Just as Carlos Peña, Alberto Unsaín and Miguel Bastón did in the dressing room, they showed me what it meant to wear the red and white stripes of Atlético Madrid. I had team-mates who did not care about the club and will never know what Atléti was really about, but I learnt a lot from the staff there. I learnt from the employees, from the former players in the veterans' association, from the delegates and the kit men, from the members of the club's senate … they're the people who help you understand the club. That's why I try to talk to the staff at Liverpool, why I try not to lose that link to the club – the real club. I think that's fundamental. I like to say hello to the cleaners, to the people on reception, to the cooks. They treat me like just another member of the team and that's exactly the way it should be. I wouldn't want them to treat me in any other way – and I wouldn't let them either.

Melwood is not a bunker. It's a training ground that's wonderfully organised. The wall that surrounds the ground is not that big, so local kids use wheelie bins to clamber up and watch training sessions;. The English press is respectful of our privacy and lets us get on with our daily work. They could easily take photos that they're not entitled to because the area is surrounded by houses that overlook the training pitches, but they respect the rules and they recognise that the day to day work we do doesn't matter to them. It's not a story.

Every Thursday we have a Family Day at Melwood. Every player is allowed to bring two people to training with him; they can watch the session and have breakfast or lunch in the canteen. It's the day when people take the opportunity to get autographs or photos. There are visits too from charities and associations for children with learning difficulties who get the chance to come and meet us. Every month, we have a meeting with the kids from the Academy too: we get together at Melwood's press room and chat with them. Then there's the people who've always been there: people like John, who comes in once a week and offers to wash your car during training; Richie, who can get you tickets for musicals and shows and brings the latest music in for the players; and Ronnie Moran, former assistant to Bob Paisley and Bill Shankly and a lovely man who likes to take a stroll round the ground.

I don't know when Melwood was built but I was told that it used to belong to St Francis Xavier school. They decided to call it Melwood after two priests at the school, Father Melling and Father Woodlock.

Sammy Lee, Rafa Benítez's assistant and one of Liverpool's historic players, told me that it's virtually the same as it was when he left the club in 1986. Technologically, it has improved, though, and now Sammy wants to change the décor. He hung up a huge mural showing some of the club's legends: Barnes, Souness, Dalglish, Gerrard, Carra, Benítez, Paisley, Shankly … I think they must be blind because they've included me, in colour, right in the middle of it. It's an honour to be part of it and I'm very grateful but quite honestly I don't deserve it. I'm going to keep on fighting and see if one day I really do deserve to be up there alongside Liverpool's chosen ones.

Sammy has also taken it upon himself to put up a plaque with the names of everyone who has ever played for the club. And, alongside photographs of the fans, he is putting up phrases uttered by Liverpool's opponents, explaining what they felt to be facing Liverpool. There is one from Johan Cruyff that takes up much of the wall in the press room, where we also meet for videos and tactical talks:

'There's not one club with an anthem like "You'll Never Walk Alone". There's not one club in the world so united with the fans. I sat there watching the Liverpool fans and they sent shivers down my spine. A mass of 40,000 people became one force behind their team. That's something not many teams have. For that I admire Liverpool more than anything.'

The first time I ever had breakfast in the canteen at Melwood, I was joined by Peter Crouch. I hardly spoke any English and we could barely talk to each other. I had arrived early to do some medical tests. After giving blood, I went up to the canteen to have a bit of juice and toast. I was a little nervous and I was surprised by how good the atmosphere was in there, by the way the captains took the new players under their wing. Gerrard came over immediately to welcome me. He patted me on the back, I turned round, stood up and shook his hand, then said: 'Good morning'. It was the only thing I knew how to say. I couldn't add another word. Steve smiled and wished me luck. He and Carra know how to ease new players into the group; they make you feel part of it right from the start.

Who you share breakfast with depends on when you arrive. When you come in, you simply sit with whoever's already there. Quite often, that will be with the lads from the reserve team, even if you've barely had the chance to speak to them before. In terms of team-building, it really works. Breakfast together and then a quick flick through the papers.

My first few weeks were far easier than I imagined. The staff really helped me. Carol and Caroline, two of the kitchen staff, would see me and immediately say 'two slices of toast', while Graham Carter, the kit man, made sure I always knew where everything was. Now I can have a decent conversation with Carol, who serves me breakfast every Thursday. While I'm signing balls and shirts, she leaves the food on the table waiting for me. She's a star. Not a day goes by without her asking after my family.

I learnt the rules bit by bit. You're not allowed to use your mobile phone outside the dressing room and you have to wear different footwear in specific parts of the complex. Three months after I first arrived, I found out that there is a separate letter box for personal letters and parcels. I had gone a few weeks wondering where my letters were, why things I was expecting hadn't reached me. I asked and they pointed out that there were two letter boxes.

I sit next to Steven Gerrard in the dressing room, because the seats and lockers are arranged in order of your shirt number. At first, Andriy Voronin sat to my right but in my second season that space went empty. What I was saying about the shoes is no joke: there is a small room on the way out to the training pitch with stacks of shelves where you have to leave your indoor shoes on the way out and your outdoor shoes on the way in, alongside the heart rate monitors we wear. It's like a beehive packed with football gear.

Because I was undergoing treatment for an ankle problem, I spent more time in the physios' room than out on the pitch during my first few days at Melwood.

Thanks to Víctor Salinas, one of the Spaniards amongst the medical staff, it was a nice experience. The treatment room is a place for making friends, learning the language and getting to know one another. It's where players get together more than anywhere else. You get to know each other in the canteen and the gym too, of course, but when you're lying on the treatment table you force yourself to speak English. The phrase 'English, please' gets repeated over and over. The physios also have a control centre, alongside the doctor's office, with a desk and computers to analyse test results. There are five treatment tables, ultrasound machines and freezers full of ice packs. That's the room where I've learnt the most English. I would go in there before or after training, listen quietly and carefully and try to understand. When Salinas couldn't treat me and I had to be looked after by one of the other English members of staff, I had no choice but to practise my English. When you're trying to tell someone about an injury, it's important to get your message across. There are lots of phrases you have to learn to make sure you get the right treatment: 'it hurts', 'it's swollen', 'it aches'.

Melwood also has a series of bedrooms where we rest on match day. English clubs don't stay in hotels the night before home games as we did in Spain. If we have a match at night, whether it's a Champions League or Premier League game, we meet at 11am and spend the day at Melwood. We take a stroll to stretch our legs, we eat, we have treatment, we rest and we listen to the manager's team talk. The rooms are small, with two beds and a table and not much else. They're bare but you don't need anything else. Since I joined Liverpool I have had a number of different room mates. Steve Finnan was the first during pre-season training in Switzerland. Then it was Momo Sissoko when we went on our Asian tour and during the season itself I shared with Peter Crouch. Last season, I started off with David N'gog during pre-season and after the campaign began I was with Yossi Benayoun. He's a fantastic room-mate. Benítez is the one who decides who shares with who. He tries to mix up experienced players with younger ones and not put the Spanish-speaking footballers together. He put me with Yossi because he knows I am more comfortable with English now. When I was at Atlético I shared with Jorge Larena for a few years, then with Antonio López and in the final season with Mariano Pernía. Personally, I prefer having individual rooms like we do with the Spanish national team but I respect the decision of the coach. Sharing helps team-building, after all.

The Player Liaison Office, run by Norman and Jane at Liverpool, is vital for any club. At Atlético Madrid, they set one up in my final season there, run by the former player Pedro Pablo. When I lived in Madrid I didn't need anyone to lend me a hand: I knew the city and the people. But when you live in an unfamiliar place or a foreign country, it's far more difficult. So much so that at first they had to go so far as to reserve me tables in restaurants. That help in making things run more smoothly is priceless. You get loads of letters you don't understand, for a start. Jane and, especially, David were vital during my first weeks in Liverpool. They speak Spanish, which really helped to speed things up, enabling me to communicate and to solve any problems I had.

'There's not one club with an anthem like "You'll Never Walk Alone". There's not one club in the world so united with the fans.

XX

A helping hand

The first person to talk to me about
him was Jorge Larena, a midfielder at
UD Las Palmas and one of my best
friends in football. I first met Jorge
when he signed for Atlético Madrid in
the summer of 2002 and we quickly
hit it off. I was on holiday in the
Canary Islands once when he told
me about a boy that he knew called
Oliver who was seriously ill and
suffering chronic problems.
I was told he was football crazy
and wanted to meet me.

The following day Jorge introduced me to a tall, slim man. His name was Benito Mayor and he was Oliver's father. Within half an hour, we were chatting to his son. He suffered from cystic fibrosis and he explained his illness to me with incredible calmness and strength of character. The conversation soon turned to football and we ended up chatting away well into the afternoon.

A few months later, the illness took hold. It was a battle our beloved Oliver couldn't win. We met one last time in Madrid, where he was being treated, and he told us that he lived every second of his life with passion. He transmitted real strength to all of us. After he passed away, Benito created the Fundación Oliver Mayor in his honour. The Foundation aims to make people aware of the human, psychological and social problems surrounding cystic fibrosis and to bring to people's attention the impact that it has on the lives not just of those who suffer the illness but their families too. The idea is to increase people's sense of solidarity and responsibility towards those that find themselves in need or at a disadvantage as a result of cystic fibrosis.

With the help of Bahía Internacional, the Fundación Oliver Mayor set up a charity football match in the summer of 2005 to raise money to help those suffering with the illness. The match was held in Las Palmas in Gran Canaria between two teams of footballers who lent their support. Jorge put together a team of friends from the Canary Islands while I tried to put together a team of friends and team-mates from within the game. Sadly, although I really wanted to play I couldn't because I was injured. At the end of the league season Spain played a World Cup qualifier against Bosnia and I ended up with a sprained ankle. I had to content myself with cheering on the team from the dugout.

Everyone was delighted to help out; it was nice to be able to assist Oliver's family. It was a wonderful occasion and the response from the Canary Islanders was magnificent. The stadium was almost full. A number of Deportivo de La Coruña players, like Manuel Pablo, Rubén Castro and Juan Carlos Valerón, were in Jorge's team. Meanwhile, my team was coached by Luis Aragonés and included Antonio Nuñez, who had just won the European Cup with Liverpool, the then Manchester United goalkeeper Ricardo, and Sergio Ramos, who was playing for Sevilla at the time before later joining Real Madrid. We won 5–2, but the result didn't matter.

For footballers, collaborating with people and organisations who aim to make others aware of the problems parts of society face is a duty. I have always tried to help out whenever I have been asked. You can't say yes to every single request because you get asked to do so many things that it's not physically possible to answer every call. But you have to try to do as much as you can. I answer letters, speak to children who are ill in hospital and do my level best not to say no to anyone who really needs help. It is vital that we help those associations and bodies with an important message to be heard.

There are lots of charities in England who work with the most needy. Christmas is the busiest time but we try to help all year round. At Christmas, Liverpool players visit ill children and take them gifts, from shirts to balls, and scarves to photos. The language barrier has prevented me from giving them as much as I would like; I would like to be able to express myself better to really engage with them and cheer them up. But the way they welcome us is always wonderful: they never stop smiling and saying thank you over and over, thousands of times, for spending some time with them …

I can still remember some of the kids I paid surprise visits to in Madrid hospitals. Some stayed silent. Others managed a nervous smile. Some never stopped chatting away. Others stared at me. Some called their family over to witness the event and pinch them to make sure it was real. But all of them displayed the same emotion: happiness. And that's something they'll never lose. It's also something that never leaves you. To be able to share that moment of happiness with them is unforgettable. I would tell them that we were looking forward to seeing them make a full recovery and coming to visit us at training to have a photo with the entire squad. That became a challenge to help them fight their illness, a goal to aim for.

I try to support as many worthy causes as I can. I backed the campaign set up by a number of newspapers in Spain after the Asian tsunami. As the advert put it, 'It doesn't take much to show solidarity to the victims of the tsunami. Simply by sending a text message with the word AYUDA [help, in Spanish] you will help many families who have been torn apart.'

But my real obsession is kids. Four or five years ago I joined the Fundación Crecer Jugando [The Growth Through Play Foundation] to help their campaign *'un jugete, una ilusión'* [toys bring hope]. I was the face of a campaign that sent toys to children from the poorest parts of the world, from Africa to Latin America, the Middle East and the Balkans. I appeared on radio and television adverts encouraging people to take part by buying special pens, spinning tops and bottles of bubble liquid. A small amount of money makes much more difference than people imagine. My messages were cut together with the stories of children who were given a toy for the first time. The idea is to reach more children from more countries every year, via the various organisations who work with children across the globe. *'Un jugete, una ilusión'* has been running since 2000 and has sent out over a million toys, as well as setting up over 800 play centres where children can go. The idea of the campaign is to remind people that playing is a fundamental right of every child, as well as a key part of a child's development and education – especially when it comes to building relationships with other children.

Along with the rest of my team-mates, I also participated with the Fundación Atlético Madrid and the Fundación López Hidalgo in the production of the Calendario Solidario 2007, a calendar designed to raise awareness and money for charity. I posed for photographs with children affected by achondroplasia and over 200,000 calendars were produced and quickly snapped up by Atlético fans. The money raised went towards the children and charities dealing with achondroplasia, which is a genetic bone disease that leads to deformities as limbs grow at uneven rates compared with the rest of the body.

One of the other charitable projects I became involved in was also designed to help children. I collaborated on a book called *Recetas Solidarias* [Charitable recipes], which was put together by the United Nations Children's Fund, UNICEF. The project involved more than just suggesting a favourite recipe for a cook book; it involved over 100 people from the world of sport, television, cinema, fashion, business, music and politics helping children. Part of the money raised from sales of the book went towards funding UNICEF programmes to guarantee human rights for boys and girls across the world.

I was asked to lend my support to a campaign called *'Día de un tren de valores'*, led by the Spanish railways. The idea was to donate one euro for every passenger who travelled on the day of the campaign. The money went towards a fund that was used for social, environmental and cultural projects, while activities were arranged such as trips for charitable organisations.

One of my most recent appearances was for the Spanish Federation for Rare Diseases *'Pacto de Todos'* campaign [All Together campaign] to raise awareness of the needs of people with rare diseases. In February 2009 they held the first World Rare Diseases Day, under the slogan: 'There are more than 3 million of us and yet still we're alone. Join the Pacto de Todos for Rare Diseases'. The idea is to stop those diseases from accounting for 35 per cent of children who die before they are a year old and 10 per cent of all those children who die between the ages of 1 and 5. We're demanding greater collaboration between everyone to try to help integrate people socially, in health, education and throughout society. With that goal in mind, FEDER are trying to show people that rare diseases affect many families.

The difficulties they face every day have led to the campaign being taken across Europe, Canada, the United States and Latin America.

I don't want to miss out the work done by Liverpool FC's Disabled Supporters' Association, who work with the club to promote accessibility to stadiums for football fans who suffer any kind of disability and help disabled fans who visit Liverpool and their carers. They're fighting to ensure that all fans have equal opportunities when it comes to enjoying football in comfort and to guarantee that disabled supporters are granted the same rights by Liverpool as all other fans.

With my friend Jorge Larena, currently at UD Las Palmas, I arranged a football match in the Canary Islands to raise funds for the Fundación de Oliver Mayor. This is the day we presented the match.

XXI

Suffering in silence

I've played with a broken rib.
The city derby against Real Madrid
was coming up and so were the
Christmas holidays but I played.
It's not that I'm a hero, it's that I
don't like missing a single match.

Fortunately, I've not had many injuries during my career. The worst I ever had was when I was a kid coming up through the youth system at Atlético Madrid, but since I've been a professional I've avoided serious setbacks. Two games stand out, though; two games I was especially disappointed to miss: the match that marked Atlético Madrid's centenary and Liverpool's visit to the Vicente Calderón in the Champions League.

When I missed the centenary game, I had picked up the only muscle injury I suffered in six years at Atlético. We were playing Osasuna on our 100th birthday. We lost 1–0. The fans packed the stadium with a sea of colour; there were spectacular mosaics, banners and ticker tape everywhere. It was a shame we couldn't mark the occasion with a victory.

Liverpool's match with Atlético at the Calderón was supposed to be my return home. Unfortunately, another muscle injury – this time picked up playing for Spain – ruled me out. There was still a week to go until the match when I was forced to go off after just fifteen minutes against Belgium. I was really looking forward to going back but you have to be very careful and very patient with muscle injuries. That was shown when I suffered another tear in the same place as I had against Birmingham a month and a half earlier.

That's why we decided it was better for me not to travel to Madrid. I would like to reiterate publicly that I'm very grateful to Atlético Madrid for inviting me to the game and proposing that I be presented with a special award – the *insignia de oro y brillantes* – in recognition of my time at the club. In the end it had to be put off and I felt sorry for the fans but it was the best thing to do. I met with Benítez, the doctors and the physios and we decided it was better for me to stay in Liverpool and work on my rehabilitation. It was such a pity not to be able to be at the Calderón. It was set to be a very special game for me but sadly it wasn't to be. I'll never forget the way the fans were that night, the brotherhood that existed between Liverpool and Atlético supporters. The way they swapped shirts and scarves … it was wonderful.

Being injured is awful. I'm not the kind of player who normally misses more than a couple of games a season through injury, so my second season at Liverpool was very strange. I hate missing games and I'm not used to it. When you get injured lots of thoughts go through your mind but one has to dominate: be patient. You have to take your time and ensure you make a full recovery. You have to work hard with the medical staff to ensure that you return to action as soon as possible but you can't rush. It's up to your body to dictate when you're ready to play again.

It's hard to explain and difficult to understand when you suffer the same injury more than once. I had only ever suffered one muscle injury at Atléti, yet at Liverpool I suffered three in as many months. It was a real hammer blow. The first time it happens you think it's normal and you keep going. The second time, you stop, you take more care and you start to ask yourself why it happened. The third time, you stop properly, you start to investigate the underlying causes and you work as hard as you can to make sure it never happens again. That was even more important in my case because it was my hamstring that was causing me problems – the muscle I live by, the one that gives you acceleration and speed. I can't take risks, so I decided to take longer than normal over my recovery to make sure we got it absolutely right. We had to be 100 per cent sure that there was no risk.

There are lots of reasons why it might have happened: I'd come off the back of a long season with the European Championships at the end of the domestic campaign; I hadn't got a good pre-season under my belt; I had enjoyed very few days off during the summer … I don't know what the main reason was but maybe I needed a longer break. I had not had much of a rest. Undergoing a proper pre-season is fundamental and it's very important to approach that work seriously because one thing's for sure: being injured for three months meant I lost things that I never got back.

The number of goals I scored went down, both in the Premier League and in Europe, I missed out on winning more caps for Spain, and when I looked back at the end of the season, I realised just how many important moments I had missed out on.

You have to be aware of those consequences during your rehabilitation: sometimes players should be more honest with themselves, we should ration our efforts better, the minutes we play; we should rest better, eat better, look after ourselves better ...

Now I know what the fans feel like when they watch us play. From the stands you see lots of things you don't notice when you're on the pitch. Watching from the side, you really suffer when you can see that the team is struggling. You'd rather be out on the pitch than helpless in a seat in the stands; you want to be there doing something about it. One thing was nice though: the reaction of the fans. It was really special to listen to the fans sing my song from the pitch; hearing it when you're not even there is comforting. I heard it once watching a game on television from home and that helps you recover: it makes you feel wanted when you're going through bad times and motivates you to work on getting fit as quickly as possible.

The worst injury I've ever suffered came before I even made it as a first team player. It happened during a training match with the youth team at Atlético. It was August, the summer of 2000. I was sixteen and I tore the tendon in my left knee. I didn't think it was particularly important at the time and I wasn't especially worried about it. I was young and didn't fully appreciate what was happening to me. It kept me out for a long time but I promised myself I would play at the

European Youth Championships in England the following May, and that kept me going. Not only did I play, we ended up as champions and I was top scorer. I even got voted player of the tournament. It didn't stop there, either: that same season, 2000–01, I made my full debut for Atlético in Spain's Second Division.

When it comes to overcoming injury there's only one method that really works: you have to work really hard with the physios. Even if it hurts. Sometimes it can feel as if their fingers are knives being plunged into your skin as they work on the injured area.

It is always frustrating to miss matches; you always want to play, you always want to help your team-mates. It's hard to take because you can see the training pitch through the windows at Melwood. You can see your team-mates out there and you're desperate to be out there with them. You get more and more anxious, more and more desperate to get back, and time seems to drag on forever. You get horribly bored. As you lie on the treatment table, you reflect on things, you resign yourself to your fate and you start to pour all your energy into working hard every day to get back into action; you try to steal back a few seconds from the clock, the odd page from the calendar. Your conversations with your team-mates change too; you try not to think about the injury.

I'd like to mention two team-mates of mine who suffered serious injuries and went through a really hard time because of them. One is Francis Durán, a Spanish reserve player at Liverpool. Just a few days after signing for Liverpool he tore his cruciate knee ligament. There were complications and he was out of action for over a year and then he tore the same ligament – but this time in the other knee. He was so unlucky but his attitude is brilliant. Every day he gives his all to come back in perfect condition, he's so determined and single-minded. You see him at Melwood and he's always smiling. His approach and mentality puts us all to shame. I really admire him. I just hope he doesn't pick up any more injuries because his response has been fantastic. I can't even begin to imagine what he has been through: here he is in a foreign country, he doesn't understand the language and he gets injured. Yet he has never been down, he has never complained, he wears a smile every day. He refuses to give in.

The other player is Juan Gómez, an Argentinian team-mate of mine at Atlético Madrid. He was one of the players who did the most to support me when I made the step up to the first team at the age of seventeen. In the penultimate game of the season against Sporting Gijón he picked up an ankle injury. It didn't seem to be especially serious but there was complication after complication until two years later he was forced to retire. He'd been beaten by an injury. He fought, he battled, but in the end he had no choice but to surrender and face the sad truth: he would never play again. His rehabilitation just didn't succeed: he never recovered the full range of movement in his foot. I would have loved to have played more games with him but it wasn't to be. I remember his brave and painful fight against adversity as a real pity, but with admiration.

Injuries are the dark side of football. You hope and pray that they will never happen to you, or at least not too often. The year that I was out because of my knee injury, having torn the tendon, was the worst I have experienced as a footballer. I was only just starting out and, fortunately, there were no lasting consequences. I made a full recovery but I do not want to live through that again.

Waiting for a diagnosis from the doctor is like waiting for an exam result. When you go into the scanner for tests on an injury, it's already too late. There's no longer anything you can do and you have no idea what's happening. There's no longer any point in worrying. What has happened has happened. That's why when they slide me into that tube, I think the best thing to do, the only thing to do, is just lie back and go to sleep.

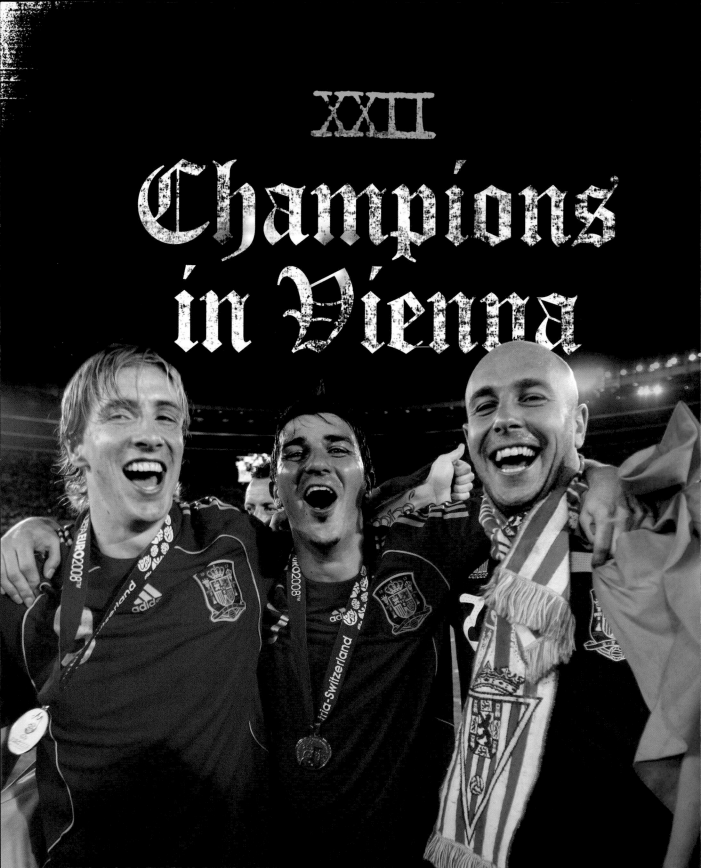

XXII
Champions
in Vienna

'Are you going to play in those boots? They're rubbish! Useless. You've got to play with aluminium studs and the longer the better! You'll slip less. And you might score more with them – you could reach a ball with longer studs.'

It was classic Luis Aragonés, one of the managers who has had the greatest impact on me throughout my career. I was with him for two seasons at Atlético Madrid and for four seasons, between 2004 and 2008, with the Spanish national team – a period he rounded off with Spain becoming European Champions in Vienna.

It was winter 2000–01 and we were at El Plantío, Burgos's stadium 250 kilometres north of Madrid, preparing for a Second Division match. In my first full season as a professional, following my brief appearance at the back end of the previous campaign, I was used to wearing boots with rubber studs. Before the match Luis, one of Atlético's former greats as a player and now in his fourth spell as coach of the club, liked to talk. And shout. About the opposition, about his own team. He stopped right in front of me. Character, personality, seeped from every pore. He called over the kit man and barked at him. 'Get *el niño* [the kid] some boots. With aluminium studs. I don't want to see him wearing rubber studs again. They're rubbish.'

No sooner said than done. Antonio Llarandi handed me another pair, this time with metal studs, just as the coach demanded. I used a spare pair that we always took with us just in case, lacing them up and going out to play. After the game, I was packing up my bag but I couldn't find my original boots. 'Antonio,' I asked, 'have you seen my boots?' The man that generation after generation of footballers had called *El Gitano* – the gypsy – looked at me and tried to stifle a laugh. 'The boss threw them in the bin.' There, in the bin in the corner of the away dressing room at El Plantío, were my boots. And there they stayed. I never wore rubber studs again.

At Atlético, Luis Aragonés didn't only show me how to act on the pitch, he showed me how to act in a dressing room too. When you're a young player you have to be the first to arrive and the last to leave. He hammered into me a real respect for my team-mates, telling me to be humble and speak as little as possible. And he made me suffer. He left me on the bench or even up in the stands. He substituted me in loads of games because he expected so much from me. When he left, I realised how important all the chats and reprimands, all the criticism and put-downs, had been for me; I realised how much he had wanted me to keep on

improving. He's a man who keeps your feet on the floor and makes you a balanced person as well as a better player. When a player starts to think about himself too much, it's the coach who brings him back down to earth, who shows him how to improve his weak points and perfect his strong ones. A coach that idolises you is useless. He has to be consistent. He always has to work to help you improve and show you that you can get better. He shouldn't tell you you're perfect – even when you score a hat-trick.

In our first season together in the Atlético dressing room, Luis was extremely insistent with me; he pushed and pushed and was always on top of me. Right from the start I was very clear in my own mind that respecting the older players and the code of the dressing room was vital, so there were times when I thought Luis was wasting time insisting on it over and over again. I already knew, I already respected those unwritten rules. There was no need to drive the point home. I'm a player who likes to take a step back, watch and learn from the rest. Back then, I barely opened my mouth, I would be the first to go in the middle for piggy-in-the-middle exercises, and I would complete every drill to the letter. I already knew it was the best way to behave as a young player at such an early stage of my career. I think Luis had developed a picture of me that was wrong.

The passage of time allows you to reflect. I think he knows that I've always responded the right way at key moments. During that 2001–02 season, I switched between being a substitute and being substituted. Luis had a lot of faith in Diego Alonso and Fernando Correa as his starting partnership up front. I had begun the season as a starter but the Youth World Cup in Trinidad and Tobago had taken me away from the team for a month to play for Spain. When I got back, the subs' bench waited. The two Uruguayans had been playing very well. Aragonés demanded a lot of me because I was very young and, I think, he wanted to build a footballer in his own image, to shape me from the dressing room to the field of play. He knew that, like him, I was an *atlético* and he wanted to mould me so that I would continue to progress.

In my second full season, by now in the top flight, everything changed. Aragonés began to use me more and I began to play better. I felt like a genuine first team player, I felt more important on the pitch and within the group. Goals came and so

I knew that a goal in the final would make me go down in history.

did an improvement in my performances. If I had deserved to be on the bench the previous season, now I was growing. I felt like people rated me more and things were coming off. Luis and I had come together at what was perhaps the most critical period in Atlético's one-hundred-year history. I remember Aragonés telling the fans that the club would need at least five years to be able to get back to where it belonged near the top of the table. He was absolutely right. He did what could have been expected of him. They brought him in to win promotion and carry out a transition in the team and at the club. He left at the end of the season, even though he still had a year left on his contract. Some had hoped that we would get straight back into Europe but he didn't think it was possible. And he was right.

We will always have a good relationship. But at the same time people always remember the fact that I was a shoo-in to be one of the three substitutes in every game. During our first season together there was a permanent tension but there

is no doubt that, just before my eighteenth birthday, the lessons that Luis handed out and his decision to constantly take me off helped me to be strong and never allow anyone to beat me. I always kept my head held high and never gave in. Sometimes it felt as if it was him or me. And yet, despite that impression, we got on very well. I never had any fights with him, we never even had an argument. Before games and during the week leading up to them he only ever had good words to say about me. But the second the referee blew the whistle, everything changed. I never asked for an explanation because I knew that the board would go up with my number on it during the first five minutes of the second half. During that season in the Second Division I knew that my matches ended when the clock hit 50 minutes. If I was sub, I knew I'd get on for 40 minutes at best. I respected his decision, though. I was too young to be trying to prove a point to anyone. I was still learning and I wasn't in a hurry. I knew that patience was a virtue – the most important virtue of all.

There were more substitutions with the national team. During the four years we were together, I was often the first man off and one particularly noticeable occasion came against Russia during the opening game of Euro 2008, when Cesc Fabregas replaced me. I was angry because after a pre-tournament match against the United States in Santander, Aragonés had told me that I had nothing to worry about and that I would be a starter in Austria. I'm not sure why he decided to tell me that – perhaps because he had taken me off at half-time in three successive pre-tournament matches against Italy, Peru and the USA. Whatever the reason, he took me off. I was angry at the time but Luis didn't say anything to me after the game against Russia and I thought that was the end of it. I never expected the media to make so much of it. Maybe that media attention was the reason Aragonés called me in and told me that as far as he was concerned it wasn't an issue. He even told me: 'Spain is Torres and ten others.'

Playing for Spain, the substitutions were constant. In my first few games under Luis I alternated substitute appearances with early departures after starting. Until, that is, a game against Belgium where I scored twice. That day I headed to the dressing room early too, having being subbed again, but it was the beginning of a process where I took a grip on a starting place.

We were in the final few games before the 2006 World Cup in Germany and in the next game I scored my first international hat-trick, against San Marino. After the match in Brussels, Luis turned round and said to me, with a glint in his eye, recalling the fact that he had subbed me again: 'I don't suppose you're angry this time.'

The atmosphere at the 2008 European Championships in Austria was fantastic. Everything ran smoothly and the first few games meant that the morale of the group grew even stronger. We beat Russia comfortably and although it was harder against Sweden we defeated them too. We overcame Greece and then came to the quarter-final against Italy. Historically, Spain have always really struggled to overcome the quarter-final hurdle but this time we cleared it, on penalties. It was a key victory for us, against a country that seemed to have the beating of us over the years and the world champions to boot. We knew that a lot of the fans expected us to go out at the quarter-final stage, but we were able to go beyond that psychological barrier to change our history. That was the moment when we realised that we could achieve anything, as was shown in the semi-final against Russia when we played without pressure, controlled the game and won comfortably. Once we had beaten Italy, we knew that we could beat anyone. Better still, we had done it while keeping faithful to our style. We had delighted the supporters too. Until then we didn't really know what was happening back in Spain but with that victory we began to realise how big it was. We saw pictures of a country that had really got behind the national team.

Having reached the semi-final of the Champions League in my first season with Liverpool, I felt like I needed to play a major final; I had been close but not quite made it. I felt like the season had ended up being slightly unfulfilling. Euro 2008 changed that. I had almost reached one final and won another.

I didn't lose any sleep over the pressure to score the winning goal in the final. I saw it as an opportunity rather than an obligation. I knew that a goal in the final would make me go down in history. Ever since 1964, people remember Marcelino, the man who scored the winning goal for Spain at the only other time the country had been European Champions. He has taken up a special place in the hearts of Spanish football fans. Before the final I had only scored one goal for Spain, against Sweden. Unlike at Liverpool where I have a greater presence in the penalty area, for Spain I peeled out to the wings more or dropped off to get involved in the play. It was a different job. And although I had only scored once, I was happy. There was one game left – and it was going to be very special.

Luis built a strong, united team that performed well even when there were players missing. That was the key to Spain's success. He imposed a winning character upon us before every game. We fought for him and for the title. We saw that he went through tough times and we wanted him to walk out of the job the way he deserved to: as a great, as a winner. He is a born motivator, someone you warm to immediately. He has a thousand anecdotes and stories from a life dedicated to the game and you learn so much from him. He won the trust of the dressing room and became one of the lads. He kept us focused and ready. Nobody hid, everybody gave their all, and we were at the peak of our game.

Luis's team-talks were legendary. The one he gave before the final was all about motivating us to go out and win. All the way through it, he called the Chelsea and Germany midfielder Michael Ballack 'Wallace'. The third time he did it, we couldn't help smiling. Like a classic Madrileño, oozing irony and cheek, ballsy as ever, Luis replied: 'I call him Wallace because I bloody well want to call him Wallace! I know perfectly well what he's called.' When we were waiting in the tunnel, ready to go out, and the tension was rising he went up to the German captain and said: 'Good luck, Wallace'. He looked at us, smiled, and winked. What a way to take the pressure off! What a character!

In the dressing room before going out to warm up, Aragonés had come up to me, looked me in the eyes and said: 'I did this with you at Atléti once, remember? Today, you're going to score twice.' With his finger he did the sign of the cross on my forehead. I honestly don't remember what happened at Atlético – I think he was right, I think I got two that day. And he was very nearly right in Austria too. I made it 1–0 and I hit the woodwork with a header.

Victory was fantastic, an unforgettable experience. I watched from the bench as the final, tense minutes ticked away. Only having a 1–0 lead meant that the game was still balanced on a knife-edge. Any dead ball or lucky break could draw Germany level. When the referee blew the final whistle, we exploded with joy. We were European Champions! We had done it! Everyone was so happy. It was a wonderful feeling. We went up to get our medals and the cup. When I reached His Majesty Juan Carlos, the King of Spain, he joked that I must be eating well in England. I looked bigger and stronger to him than I had done when I left for Liverpool. A few minutes later Uefa president Michel Platini handed the trophy that crowned us European Champions to our captain Iker Casillas.

Surrounded by photographers, the lap of honour was incredible. Draped in flags, we didn't know whether to walk or run or leap round the pitch. I found my way across to the stands and looked for my family. They were waiting for me, delighted. I clambered over seats to reach them and took the kisses and hugs of those people who have always been there for me back to the dressing room with me. What awaited was incredible. The King and Queen of Spain and the Prince and Princess of Asturias came down to the dressing room to congratulate us and really joined in – it was is if they were part of the team too. They spoke to everyone and congratulated us on behalf of the whole country. I was really impressed by them and they seemed to genuinely enjoy themselves. All the while, bit by bit, what we had just achieved was starting to dawn on us.

The best was yet to come. The party on the plane, with the trophy as guest of honour, was the start of a fantastic, exciting night. When we arrived at Barajas airport in Madrid, the staff greeted us like heroes; they were all going crazy. And that was just the beginning. On the bus on the way into Madrid I could not believe my eyes. I never imagined that people would react like that, that there would be so many fans waiting for us.

As we were just coming into the city, a fan shouted 'Torres, catch!' and threw me a Spain flag with the Atlético badge in the middle of it. It accompanied me for the rest of the journey on that open-topped bus.

When we reached the Plaza de Colón in central Madrid, there were so many people waiting for us that we couldn't believe it. People had gone crazy. After Pepe Reina's memorable performance with the microphone, when he introduced the players one by one and led the singing, the party continued long into the night. Too long. I'd only had a couple of hours sleep when we arrived for a formal reception at the Royal Palace and then travelled from there to visit the Prime Minister.

Then there was Aragonés. He bid farewell in the best possible way: with the European Championship trophy under his arm. He did the right thing by going. Now, nothing can take away his success. He also set the ball rolling, creating a successful team ready for the South Africa World Cup in 2010. He brought a new generation through and he should be remembered for that. He will be missed as a person and a coach. He likes to control every little detail and build a real unit, a good, close-knit group of players and staff. And even now, no Spain get-together is complete without someone remembering one of Luis's moments as the Spanish coach. Isn't that right, lads?

XXIII
On the podium in Zurich

There I was, up there with the best. I felt a real sense of pride – and gratitude towards everyone who'd helped to get me there, who'd made it possible for me to enjoy a special day in Zurich.

It was a wonderful feeling to open the newspaper and read: 'Fernando Torres came third in the 2008 FIFA World Player Award held in the Zurich Opera House. The No. 9 secured his place amongst football's elite thanks to the 203 points he collected in the votes cast by coaches and captains of the 208 football federations that make up FIFA. The winner was Cristiano Ronaldo with 935 points and Leo Messi came second with 678 points, while Kaká (on 183) and Xavi Hernández (on 155) came fourth and fifth respectively. The result mirrors that of *France Football*'s European Footballer of the Year award, which was announced a month ago. Yet more recognition for the Madrid-born footballer who has found himself amongst the best players in the world after a season packed with success and crowned by scoring the historic winning goal for Spain against Germany in the final of Euro 2008. Premier League Player of the Year at the Northwest Awards, third in the Ballon d'Or, a member of the FIFPro team of

the season, fans' Player of the Year at Liverpool ... just reward for a season of success and hard work with Liverpool and the Spanish national team.'

Someone told me that only one Spanish player has been amongst the top three at the FIFA World Player Award since its inauguration in 1991 – Raúl González who, like me, was third in 2001. At proud moments like that, you think of those who've helped you along the way and who share in your success, especially your family. My parents and my brother and sister had to get up early for me, they gave up their spare time, they missed work, they missed classes at school and university. It's thanks to their sacrifices that we've been able to enjoy nights like the one in Zurich together. My girlfriend has always been at my side, supporting me and putting up with the bad times that every sportsman goes through. And then of course there are my friends and teammates, the coaches and everyone at Atlético Madrid – the people who helped me take my first steps in football. People like Rangel, Pedro Calvo, Arganda, Abraham; everyone at Bahia Internacional, the company that has looked after me since I was fifteen, advising me, taking care of me and teaching me throughout my career. All of them contributed to getting me to Switzerland, and it was thanks to them that I could enjoy such a wonderful experience.

I felt like a gatecrasher at someone else's party. 2008 was a wonderful year, both for me as an individual and for the teams I played for: Liverpool and the Spanish national team, who won the European Championships. Above all, it was Euro 2008 that saw me take my place alongside the best in the world at the gala in Switzerland.

Just being there was an honour. I remember watching those events when I was a kid and it felt like something from another galaxy, reserved for the chosen ones: Van Basten, Rivaldo, Figo, Ronaldo, Zidane, Ronaldinho … I never dreamed I'd be one of the chosen ones; I never even thought I'd get close to them. I thought it was impossible.

Everything changed when Liverpool gave me the chance to compete at the highest level. The success of my debut season with Liverpool and the extraordinary finale to the European Championships took me to Zurich. I'd enjoyed a wonderful season in the red of Liverpool and it was rounded off perfectly in the red of Spain. My goal in the final made a huge difference when it came to fighting for the title of 2008's best player. But I look upon the months at Liverpool as the ones that really let me aspire to a place amongst the ten most important footballers in the world. It was an unforgettable year at Anfield; all that was missing was a title that would have rounded it off perfectly – and maybe earned me a few more votes in Zurich.

The favourites were pretty obvious. Cristiano Ronaldo was a worthy winner. It was clear from the moment we arrived in Zurich that two men were some way ahead of the rest: Messi was the only other genuine candidate alongside Ronaldo. Below them were Xavi, Kaká and me. We knew that we were fighting for bronze. Xavi and I were the new boys; the others had all been here before. It was an intense day, packed with interviews, press conferences and the presentation of the nominees, of travelling back and forth between the hotel and the Opera House. A wonderful occasion; a night to remember and to enjoy.

Cristiano had the best year, both individually and collectively. Nobody doubted that he would win – not even him. Messi had been injured for quite a while early in the season, which didn't help his cause. Also, I think that to be a serious contender he needed to win something for Barcelona and that didn't happen. It's true that he won an Olympic gold with Argentina and that he was extraordinary at the end of the year but Cristiano had won the Premier League, the Champions League and the European Golden Boot. The only thing you could hold against him was Euro 2008, but that would be unfair. Overall, he had been the best.

As for Kaká, he's a unique player, winner of the award the previous year. No one could deny that he deserved his place alongside the greats. Milan might not have had a great season but he is a footballer who always offers so much.

Xavi also deserved to be recognised after he had been the best player at Euro 2008 and contributed to Barcelona reaching the Champions League semi-final. He perhaps had more of a role to play collectively than I did but the goal in the final made me stand out. The fact that five Spaniards were amongst the top ten was very satisfying. I don't think anything like that had ever happened before: Spain had more players in the top ten than any other country. Although none of us won the award, we were all there and hopefully the national team can continue to be successful in the future. Next time, maybe a Spaniard will be FIFA World Player of the Year or Ballon d'Or winner. For now, we have to keep working and winning trophies with club and country. After all, it's success with your team that ultimately brings success as an individual. We owed our presence at the gala in Zurich to our team-mates.

The way that the event was organised was extraordinary. We couldn't have asked for more; we were treated wonderfully. To be able to chat about football to Pelé, Beckenbauer, Matthäus, Platini or Butragueño was fantastic. Swapping stories with them was a dream. Platini, for example, was busy reminiscing about the 1984 European Championship final in which he played for France against Spain. He talked about what a great tournament Spain had. Like the rest of us, he thought they deserved to be European Champions back then. At the time everyone talked about Luis Arconada's mistake in the final; Spain's goalkeeper had handed Platini the trophy. At Euro 2008 fate intervened and, as Uefa president, Platini had to hand the trophy to Spain's goalkeeper, Iker Casillas.

Throughout the ceremony, the president of the Spanish Football Federation, Ángel María Villar, was sitting next to me; Barcelona president Joan Laporta came over to congratulate me and so did Txiki Beguiristain, Barcelona's sporting director who was there with the Barça players. All around us were great players from the history of the game. I never imagined I would spend an evening in such company. I felt so privileged. Just being amongst the top five was the business. Winning it must be unbelievable.

I tried to make sure that I kept my feet on the ground all the time. I think that's why I enjoyed it so much. I said to myself: this is such a wonderful moment, I have to come back again. I would love to return but I also know that to do so I will have to work extremely hard. One opportunity might come with the 2010 World Cup in South Africa. If Spain can win the tournament, then there is a good chance that a Spaniard will be up there on the podium. Before that, though, come nine months of football with Liverpool as we fight to win trophies. Scoring goals helps gather votes too; if I can have a good season with my club and round it off with international success, then there's a genuine hope of returning to Zurich.

But the truth is I don't know what to think. I don't know whether I should agree with Kelly Smith who, when Ronaldo was proclaimed the winner, whispered in my ear: 'Relax, next year it will be you.' Or whether I should stick by my own initial reaction when I saw the photograph of the nominees and thought to myself: 'Bloody hell, where's Steven Gerrard?'

XXIV

Switching off

It's not easy living abroad, especially when it's the first time you've been away from home. That's why I was determined to make the right decision when it came to finding somewhere to live: I knew I would spend more time at home than anywhere else.

In the end, we chose a house fifty yards from where Pepe Reina lives with his family. When you arrive somewhere for the first time, it helps to be able to learn from someone who has been there longer than you and has been through the same process you'll have to go through. You have to get used to a new country, a new currency and a new climate, so you have to feel comfortable in your new home.

We've been supported by Pepe and his family and the results of that can be seen out on the pitch. When all you have to worry about is the football, when you don't have a million other things going round your head and you're relaxed and comfortable in your day-to-day life, your performances improve. The demands made on players in England are huge. You have to win every game and you can't afford to be wasting time thinking about anything else when it comes to match day.

Reina told me that when he arrived he was lucky enough to have the support of the former Liverpool striker Fernando Morientes. That made everything easier for him. The support we received made us feel happy and comfortable right from the start and made adapting to life in England much easier. I have always seen life as a case of give and take so I've tried to do things the right way and show a willingness to learn. It's important to listen and accept the advice that people who have lived through the same experience can offer you.

As I said, I'm very much a homely person. I am at my most comfortable and relaxed there. In my case it's true what they say: there's no place like home. My normal day is much the same as any sportsman's. I travel to Melwood for training every morning and have my breakfast there with the rest of the players. After training on the pitch there's a gym session and treatment with the physios, then it's home for lunch. I still take a siesta after eating, while my body digests lunch – there are some Spanish customs that I haven't left behind. I don't sleep all afternoon but as a sportsman I am conscious that after a tough session the most important thing is to eat well and rest. That's the best way to refuel and recover.

I'll eat anything, especially meat fresh from the barbeque. I don't spend hours in the kitchen, although I used to do quite a lot of cooking when I was in Madrid. When I got back from training, Olalla would be studying and I would prepare

lunch. It got to be quite a hobby. I was no expert but I could do decent lentils, pasta, Spanish tortilla, soups and hot dogs. There was the occasional disaster, of course, but I felt comfortable as the house chef. Bit by bit, though, I lost the bug. I started cooking less and shopping more.

We have adapted perfectly to Liverpool but when it comes to eating we still follow a Spanish timetable. Eating at English times still feels too early so we started arranging barbeques. A few of us got together along with Mikel Arteta from Everton, who's a good friend, and prepared some meat. It's a good excuse to spend time with your friends and have some fun. Normally we meet at Pepe Reina's house or at mine. One Sunday, we started eating in the garden. It was a sunny day with the odd cloud and we didn't think anything of it ... until the heavens opened and it started snowing. Yes, snowing! Since then, the slightest sign of bad weather and we set up in the garage instead.

I enjoy shopping, too. A friend of mine in Liverpool sometimes opens up his shop for me so that I can go when it's quiet. Then there's the obligatory trip to the supermarket to make sure the fridge is well stocked. I like to stroll around the big department stores. You always find something new for the house or the latest fashions in décor and clothing. I don't suffer the same amount of hassle in England as I did in Spain and I can go about my business much more easily. I'm not worried about anyone and pretty much no one is worried about me.

During my first few months in Liverpool, I seemed to be permanently surrounded by hammers, screwdrivers, pliers and spanners as I discovered a new hobby: putting together furniture. There were tools everywhere.

In Spain I hadn't put together a single wardrobe but here in England I found myself in the position where I either had to get on and do it or the box would just gather dust. I can be pretty determined and once I start something I have to get it finished as soon as possible. Sometimes, I would end up getting so irritated I would end up crawling to bed shattered – but with the work done. Bit by bit I started to learn the tricks of the trade and I was improving all the time.

My determination to finish the job off meant that one night in 2007 I didn't finish until the small hours. I had come home in a bad mood after we had lost 1–0 at home to Olympique Marseilles in the Champions League. I decided the best way to work the frustration out of my system was to put together two pieces of furniture for the living room. By the time I had finished it was 4am.

One my favourite moments each day, matches permitting, is the evening stroll with Olalla and our two dogs. They're English bulldogs, a male called Pomo and a female called Llanta. They have been living with us for a few years and made the journey to Liverpool with us. It's nice to stroll round quiet places with them – we have found a couple of parks near where we live that are relaxed and peaceful, offering a real escape.

At home, we spend time playing board games with friends and family. When it comes to Monopoly, Scatergory, or Hotel, there are real battles. For a change, we sometimes play cards, even though I'm not one for the typical footballer's games like poker or the games played with a 40-card Spanish deck, like *mus* or *pocha*. But I do enjoy playing *brisca* and *tute*, Spanish games similar to trumps. I don't know if people play these in England but in Spain they're a hit amongst older people, like our grandparents.

And then of course there are the football matches on the PlayStation. I spent hours playing in Madrid but I'm losing the habit in Liverpool. I have, though, developed a taste for surfing the internet. I couldn't claim to be a computer expert but I know what I'm doing when it comes to buying things online or using the net to check out the sports news at home and abroad – the normal stuff.

Cinema, television and books also take up my time. I prefer films where the plot is believable, where it feels like the storyline is credible. There aren't many of them, though, so I don't watch a huge amount of films – except to help me learn the language. I read all sorts of books. When you're travelling with the team a book is the best friend you can have. Because I'm quite impatient, once I start a book I have to finish it, and as soon as possible. I can't put the book down. I just can't stop. The same happens with television series. I devour episode after episode when I'm in hotels and travelling with my team or the Spanish squad.

Television is an alternative and I like to be up to date with what's going on in the world, and not just the sports news. My favourite programmes are the *Dog Whisperer* and *Supernanny*. I also watch *Callejeros*, which is a Spanish programme, based on reports about people who live on the margins of society and how they adapt to life on the streets. The truth is that I don't watch much English television, although I am addicted to Sky Sports.

As for music, I'm trying to complete the collection of those groups who've made an impact on me over the years. On my last birthday I was given the complete sets of Nirvana and Joaquín Sabina, a famous Spanish singer. I also want to get together all the records brought out by Andrés Calamaro and Duncan Dhu. When I look back I think of the songs my brothers used to listen to. Spanish pop groups like Hombres G and Los Rodríguez still play in my mind.

XXV

I'll never walk alone

It's quiet in the tunnel. You're ready to go out onto the pitch. The tension grows. The atmosphere closes in. The noise comes from the stands. No one talks. All you can hear is the eternal sound of the song that accompanies Liverpool wherever they go.

'hen you walk through a storm, hold you head up high, and don't be afraid of the dark...' It's a beautiful moment. We're used to it now but Liverpool's opponents go out onto the pitch already a goal down. Our fans never underestimate anyone, but right from the start their confidence rubs off on you. With them there, you know you'll never walk alone.

In Spain, the matches that are really special for us Atlético Madrid fans are the ones against Real Madrid. In England, it's against Everton and Manchester United that the decibels climb. Tradition is everything and there is respect too: the Kop never forgets Liverpool's former players. They are remembered forever and if they return to Anfield they are always greeted with a huge and heartfelt ovation, a sign of the fans' gratitude – even if they are wearing another team's shirt. When you see it on television you don't realise how emotional it can be; when you're on the pitch, you do. Sometimes I look around and see the fans standing to applaud a former Red and I find that incredible. I'd love to be able to witness it from the stands one day.

When I look towards the stands one of the things that always strikes me is the way the older fans behave – the veterans of countless Liverpool games. These are people who come up to me and ask how I am, how my family is getting on in England, or how I feel after a game. My relationship with the fans is closer than it was in Spain. I have to admit that at first I was cautious about the fans. I was reluctant to get too close. In Madrid, I was often a bit defensive because the pressure of popularity and fame could be overwhelming. Sometimes I needed tranquillity. I had to get away from football and disconnect but it was really difficult because the fans didn't leave you alone for a minute. They would come up to you and say the first thing that came into their head. In Liverpool, I started the same way – distant, cold. But with every passing day I began to realise that English people have a different character to Spaniards. Lots of them are happy enough with a simple smile. They respect you completely. The same is true during the games. The subs' benches at Liverpool are right in amongst the fans. There are men and women, 60 or 70 years old, sitting right next to us, barely 50 centimetres away. But they never cross the line. They always show real respect and they let you follow the game with the intensity that you'd expect from the dugout.

Liverpool fans are proud of the fact that they're special. They're proud of that respect. Everton fans also walk with their heads held high. You often see blue and red shirts mixed in together in the stands and there is always a great atmosphere; there's a sense of brotherhood, of good humour, friendship and harmony. There are plenty of families that are divided by their colours but united by everything else. It's strange: despite the huge rivalry there is between Liverpool and Everton, there is respect and unity, a family feel about the football. I don't know what it is that makes some choose to worship at Anfield and others at Goodison Park, but I'm sure that family traditions play a part in the love and loyalty that supporters show their clubs.

In Spain Atlético's fans are the best. They are my people and always have been. But the big difference between the Vicente Calderón and Anfield is that at Anfield you never hear a single bad word from your own supporters. The very worst you'll ever hear is a murmur, a rumble of discontent – and that never lasts more than a few seconds.

The Kop is magical and generous; it transmits a kind of positive energy that fills you with confidence. It never lets you down. It never leaves you.

Liverpool's fans appreciate the effort you make and are quick to reward you for it. Sometimes, when things are going badly, when you're having a terrible night, you almost feel like turning round to them and saying: 'Whistle us! Boo us! We're playing so badly!' That's one of the reasons why it hurts even more when things don't go well. You return to the dressing room having given everything. You can barely breathe. And you do it for them, because they deserve it. Liverpool's fans are incredible.

One of the English traditions that the Spanish have started to copy in recent years is to go to the stadium in your team's colours. Everyone, from the youngest to the oldest, is decked out in the team's colours. Everything's red: shirts, scarves, hats, gloves, flags, tracksuits, everything ... it's as if the stands have been dressed up for a party. I also get sent things by fans all the time; gifts arrive virtually every day. I get photographs, collages, cuttings, toys, wigs, framed pictures, t-shirts with slogans printed on them, wrist bands ... I could run my own souvenir shop with the things that arrive. Not that I'd ever sell any of it: I'm aware of how much effort they have made to buy things in shops or to make things for me. There's not always space for it all but I keep everything and look upon the things that are sent to me with fondness and gratitude.

It's hard to explain how I feel when the fans chant my name, but I'm going to try. In the first few games I played they sang my surname like they used to do with Dalglish and Fowler. They clapped their hands and then chanted *To-rres* just as they once finished off with *Dal-glish* or *Fow-ler*. I'd been told that it's special when the Kop dedicate a song to you. When I found out that they were using the same one as they had used with the club's No. 1 player of all time, Kenny Dalglish, and one of the greatest strikers in the history of Anfield, Robbie Fowler, I felt very proud. But I also felt a real sense of responsibility because they're associating you with the legends of Liverpool. These guys were everything to this club and always will be. I felt very proud to be treated just as they were.

But it's not just about the chant. Even before I began my first season I saw lots of boys and girls wearing Liverpool shirts with my name and number. From Hong Kong to Rotterdam, where we played during pre-season in 2008, from Toulouse for the Champions League qualifier to Birmingham where we faced Aston Villa on the

opening day, I saw them. I felt genuinely wanted. I hadn't given them anything yet and they were already giving me so much. I arrived as the most expensive signing in the club's history and with an enormous weight of responsibility on my shoulders. But I knew there and then that I'd made the right decision.

Their welcome eased my first steps as a Liverpool player. I felt like I'd lived in England all my life, like I had always been a Liverpool player.

Then there was the song. My song. Owen Brown, who looks after the players at Anfield, sent me a message to tip me off that the Kop was preparing a musical tribute to me. He told me that they were going to sing it to the tune of 'When Johnny Comes Marching Home'; what he wouldn't tell me were the words. I didn't give it any more thought until one day, I heard it, coming from the stands:

'His armband proved he was a red, Torres, Torres.
You'll never walk alone it said, Torres, Torres.
We bought the lad from sunny Spain
He gets the ball he scores again
Fer-nan-do Torres, Liverpool's number nine.'

Not many fans sang the song that day because most of them didn't know the words yet. But by the following week, you could make it out pretty clearly and it grew and grew until virtually everyone sang it. Sometimes, it feels like they must have sung it a hundred times a game. It's incredible. I can't thank them enough.

The words are brilliant, almost unbelievable, and so is the story behind it. It all starts with the captain's armband my friends gave me when I was still in Madrid, with 'We'll Never Walk Alone' written on the inside. The Liverpool fans have always taken that as a sign that I was one of them all along; so they wanted everyone else

to know it too and they wanted me to feel like a true Red. They've succeeded. I feel a genuine affection towards Liverpool. One of these days I might just surprise my friends by getting a tattoo that says We'll Never Walk Alone ... That photo revealing the armband proved to be a premonition. I never imagined that one day life would lead me to Liverpool.

The bad moments that Liverpool's fans have suffered have made them even stronger. I was fortunate enough to score two against Blackburn on Saturday 11 April 2009. I celebrated by pointing to the heavens. Those two goals were dedicated to the fans who lost their lives at Hillsborough and to their families. It was twenty years since the tragedy and I knew that it was a special game for those families, just four days before the anniversary.

If that match at Anfield was a very important day for all Liverpool fans, what followed a few days later was unforgettable. As I arrived through the players' entrance and came out into the stadium, I could hardly believe what I was seeing. The stadium was almost full to commemorate the twentieth anniversary of Hillsborough; the Kop was packed and the main stand and centenary stand were full too. More than 35,000 people were there. The day before we had drawn 4–4 with Chelsea in the Champions League at Stamford Bridge. That had been a memorable occasion, but the reception we got at Anfield gave me goose bumps. All of our fans stood up and gave us an ovation that seemed to go on for ages. The memorial for those who lost their lives sent a shiver through me. The families of those who died are still demanding justice for the 96 and they also wanted to celebrate their lives.

They will never be forgotten. Twenty years later, for many the tears are still tears of anger.

I spoke to a couple of supporters who had been in Sheffield on the afternoon of the catastrophe. They told me that they are still gripped by fear and pain. What happened that day is still engraved in their minds. Children and the old dying, imprisoned behind metal bars, while others, unaware of what was happening, kept pushing to get into the stadium and see the game. When you think about it, it's terrifying. It's awful. The unity between the players and the fans comes in part from having lived that terrible experience together. At the anniversary, Kenny Dalglish led a prayer for all the fans from the altar; it took him over a minute to begin, such was the ovation he was given. He was the manager in Sheffield that day. Then a respectful silence brought an end to an emotional, difficult and heartfelt occasion.

Whenever there is a minute's silence in England's football stadiums it is impeccably observed. It is a minute that goes straight to the heart; a tear puncturing the silence. Can you imagine the Atlético Madrid hymn playing at the Santiago Bernabéu in honour of a child who'd died? I can't. But there were Everton fans at Anfield on that anniversary day who listened in respectful silence, without uttering a single word. It could only happen in England.

PHOTOGRAPHIC ACKNOWLEDGEMENTS

All photographs courtesy of Jose Antonio Garcia Sirvent with the exception of the following: pages 28-29: AFP/Getty Images; page 66: Action Images/Sporting Pictures; pages 78-79: Barry Coombs/EMPICS; page 82 left: Action Images/Michael Regan; page 82 right: Action Images/Carl Racine; page 108: AP Photos/Paul Thomas; page 118: AFP/Getty Images; pages 132-133: Getty Images; page 136: AP Photos/Themba Hadebe; page 138: AP Photos/Fernando Bustamante; pages 160, 162, 166-167: Action Images/Michael Regan; page 170: Reuters/Mark Noble; pages 174-175, Action Images/Jason Cairnduff; page 176: Peter Byrne/Press Association; page 179: Action Images/Reuters/Peter Noble; page 182: AP Photos/Luca Bruno; pages 186-187: AP Photos/Antonio Calanni; pages 190-191: AP Photos/Matt Dunham; pages 194-195: AP Photos/John Super; pages 200-201: AP Photos/Paul Thomas; page 213: Reuters/Phil Noble; page 214: Action Images/ Jason Cairnduff; page 217: AP Photos/Bernat Armangue; pages 228-229, 234-235: Peter Byrne/Press Association; pages 242-243: Reuters/Christian Charisius; page 254: Adam Davy/EMPICS; page 259: EMPICS. Endpapers: Neal Simpson/EMPICS.